Delicious Detox
Fast and Easy Recipes to Boost Energy and Improve Health

Carol Morley, ND

Library and Archives Canada Cataloguing in Publication

Morley, Carol, 1976-
Delicious detox : fast and easy recipes to boost energy and improve
health / Carol Morley

Includes index.
ISBN 978-0-9865517-0-3

1. Cookery (Natural foods). 2. Food allergy--Diet therapy--Recipes.
3. Detoxification (Health). 4. Cookery. I. Title.

TX741.M653 2010   641.5'63   C2010-901118-X

Cover and interior design by Kerri Kenny
Photography by Alexis Nilsen, Kerri Kenny, and Carol Morley
Edited by Andrea Lemieux
Index by Judith Brand

Otterville Press
404–201 City Centre Drive
Mississauga, ON
L5B 2T4

info@ottervillepress.com

Printed and bound in Canada
Printed on acid-free paper
Sixth Print

Contents

Acknowledgements

This cookbook is the culmination of many years of study, clinical experience, inspiration, and dedication. I am indebted to the many people who have helped shaped my career and my philosophy in treating patients and in life.

Thank you to my sister, Angela, who is always there to make me laugh and listen to a lecture from me on eating healthfully.

A special thank you to my parents. Dad, for teaching me and showing me what work ethic really means. Mom, for creating the cook I am today. This cookbook is a reality because of your Puréed Mung Bean Soup, the soup that proved detox can be delicious. What would I have done without your food packages throughout my years at McMaster and CCNM?

And, of course, my husband and sous-chef, Chris, who has tasted the good, the bad, and the ugly over the years. You remind me that not everyone knows what kale is and that removing wheat from one's diet for three weeks is not as easy as I think it is. You inspire me to cook with love.

Preface

It's been over a decade since I did my first detox. In 1999, when I was a first-year student at the Canadian College of Naturopathic Medicine, I embarked on three weeks of clean, healthful eating.

I set aside wheat, dairy, sugar, caffeine, alcohol, and red meat. After a few days, I had more energy, a clearer mind, and better digestion. As the detox continued, I felt better and better and have never looked back.

I've now done dozens of detoxes. And as a practising naturopathic doctor, I regularly recommend that patients do a three-week detox as part of their treatment plan. It helps my patients improve their health, lose weight, and identify the foods that are possibly contributing to their medical problems.

A detox is a time to give your body a break, an opportunity to reconnect with healthful foods and help you feel better. With the help of this book, you'll have the knowledge to start a three-week detox or simply introduce healthier foods to your family's dinner table.

Delicious Detox answers the two questions I'm most frequently asked: If I go on a detox, what can I eat? And will it taste any good?

I've tried each of these recipes in my own kitchen. I've prepared these meals for my family and shared many of the recipes with my patients.

This is your guide to eighty recipes that are easy to prepare and delicious to eat.

Detox Basics

Should I Start a Detox?

Detoxification is a wonderful way to help your body function at its best, but it is not for everyone. If you are suffering an acute flare-up of a chronic condition, are actively fighting infection or illness, or are pregnant or nursing, you should not begin a detox program. There are many other ways to support your body at this time.

Talk with your naturopathic doctor to find out if a detox is right for you, or to find alternative methods of improving your health. Because there are so many different kinds of detox programs, it is important to find one that suits you the best.

What Is Allowed on the Delicious Detox?

Below is the list of the foods that can and can't be consumed during the three-week detox. Please check with your naturopathic doctor for an individual list tailored to your health concerns.
Make sure to drink at least eight cups (two litres) of water every day, and start your day with a glass of warm water with a squeeze of fresh lemon.

	YES	NO
PROTEINS	• CHICKEN, TURKEY • FISH • BEANS (CHICKPEAS, LENTILS ADZUKI, ETC.)	• BEEF, LAMB, PORK • GOAT • EGGS • SHELLFISH • SOY
WHOLE GRAINS & FLOURS	• GLUTEN-FREE GRAINS SUCH AS QUINOA, AMARANTH, MILLET, BUCKWHEAT, and BROWN RICE • GLUTEN-FREE FLOURS • GLUTEN-FREE PASTA (BROWN RICE, QUINOA, ETC.) • PLAIN BROWN RICE CAKES and CRACKERS	• WHEAT, RYE, BARLEY • OATS • SPELT • KAMUT • WHITE or WHOLE-WHEAT FLOURS

	YES	NO
VEGETABLES	• MOST VEGETABLES	• TOMATOES, EGGPLANT, WHITE POTATOES • CORN • MUSHROOMS
FRUITS	• MOST FRUITS	• ORANGES • BANANAS • MELONS • DRIED FRUIT • FRUIT JUICES
NUTS, SEEDS & OILS	• UNSALTED RAW ALMONDS, WALNUTS, BRAZIL NUTS, PECANS • ALMOND BUTTER and OTHER NUT BUTTERS • PUMPKIN SEEDS, SUNFLOWER SEEDS, FLAXSEEDS, SESAME SEEDS • EXTRA - VIRGIN OLIVE OIL, SUNFLOWER OIL, SESAME OIL	• PEANUTS or PEANUT BUTTER • PEANUT OIL, CORN OIL, VEGETABLE OIL, CANOLA OIL • BUTTER • MARGARINE
EXTRAS	• RICE MILK, ALMOND MILK • HERBAL TEAS, GREEN / WHITE TEA, ROOIBUS TEA • SEA SALT • ALL HERBS and SPICES	• ALCOHOL • CAFFEINE • SUGAR • VINEGAR • DAIRY (MILK, CHEESE, YOGURT, ETC.) • MSG, PRESERVATIVES, SULPHITES

Preparation Is Key

Preparation is key, whether you are on a detox or not. Eating healthfully takes time and organization, even for the most seasoned "healthy eater." Having one day to organize, go grocery shopping, and prepare properly will set you off on the right foot when planning to do a three-week detox. When you are a busy person with little time to cook during the week, making a few quick dishes before you actually start can be a huge time saver.

One of the major obstacles is not having a stocked pantry and fridge. Nothing can be more frustrating! Use the shopping lists below to ensure you have all the right spices and oils in your pantry. Of course, you could eat steamed veggies, brown rice, and baked chicken for the entire three weeks, leaving your preparation very simple. You could also prepare two big batches of soup at the beginning and just eat soup for lunch every day. However, the point of this book is to make your detox more interesting
— and flavourful.

Based on the weekly shopping lists and fourteen-day meal planner that follow, here are some good to-do lists to guide you as you embark on your delicious detox adventure! The first list will prepare you for your first week.

1. Make the Basic Hummus (page 86).
2. Cook 2 cups (500 mL) of dried adzuki beans, which will make about 5 cups (1.25 L) cooked adzuki beans. One and one-half cups (375 mL) will be used for the Warm Spicy Sweet Potato Salad, 1½ cups (375 mL) will be used for the Adzuki Bean and Squash Sauté, and the rest can be frozen to be used at a later date.
3. Make the Warm Spicy Sweet Potato Salad (page 25).
4. Boil the beets.
5. Make the Parsley Pesto (page 88).
6. Make the Adzuki Bean and Squash Sauté (page 53).
7. Make the Easy Roast Chicken (page 38).
8. Make and freeze some chicken stock using leftovers from the Easy Roast Chicken.

For the second week, make yourself another to-do list, go grocery shopping again, and prep a few different things.

1. Make the Basic Hummus (page 86).
2. Make the Chickpea Slaw (page 22).
3. Make the Tuna and Salmon Salad (page 29).
4. Make the Squash Soup (page 33) and freeze it in individual portions.
5. Make the spice mixture for the Blackened Whitefish (page 48)
    and the Crunchy Chicken Nuggets (page 41).

To plan your meals for the third week, you can repeat dishes from the first two weeks as well as try some new recipes. Take stock of all your pantry items, noting which ones need restocking, and make yourself a new shopping list and a new meal planner, using the preceding ones as templates.

Weekly Shopping Lists

The shopping lists below are for each of the first two weeks of your detox.
The quantities given are enough for two people.

Week 1

Proteins

1 (5-pound / 2.2 kg) roasting chicken
2 (19-ounce / 540 mL) cans chickpeas
2 (15-ounce / 450 mL) cans adzuki beans, or 3 cups (750 mL) dried adzuki beans
1 cup (250 mL) dried red lentils
1 (19-ounce / 540 mL) can white kidney beans
1 (6-ounce / 170 g) can chunk light tuna
2 salmon steaks
1 large rainbow trout fillet
4 boneless, skinless chicken breasts

Whole Grains

3 cups (750 mL) long-grain brown rice
1 cup (250 mL) quinoa
¾ cup (175 mL) amaranth
Brown rice flour (about 1 cup / 250 mL)
1 (16-ounce / 500 g) package brown rice pasta
1 (4.47-ounce / 127 g) package plain unsalted brown rice cakes
1 (3.5-ounce / 100 g) package sesame brown rice crackers

Veggies and Fresh Herbs

3 yellow onions
3 fennel bulbs
6 large carrots
3 sweet potatoes
1 butternut squash
1 acorn squash
2 bunches of kale
1 red pepper
1 green pepper
2 yellow peppers
1 zucchini
1 bunch of broccoli
1 bunch of celery
1 bunch of asparagus
1 head of romaine lettuce

1 to 2 bags fresh spinach
   (about 6 cups / 1.5 L)
14 small beets
1 English cucumber
2 jalapeño peppers
3 avocadoes
1 red onion
2 shallots
3 garlic bulbs
1 (3-inch / 8 cm) piece
   of fresh gingerroot
1 bunch of parsley
1 bunch of cilantro
1 bunch of sage
1 bunch of thyme

Fruits

6 lemons
3 limes
1 fresh pineapple
1 pint (500 mL) fresh blueberries
1 (21-ounce / 600 g) package frozen strawberries
1 (21-ounce / 600 g) package frozen blueberries
2 pears
5 apples
1 mango

Nuts, Seeds, and Oils

¼ cup (60 mL) slivered raw almonds
1½ cups (375 mL) raw walnuts
½ cup (125 mL) sesame seeds
1 cup (250 mL) flaxseeds
3 tablespoons (45 mL) pumpkin seeds

1 (8-ounce / 250 g) jar almond butter
1 (8-ounce / 250 g) jar tahini
   (sesame seed butter)
1 (16-ounce / 500 mL) bottle
   flaxseed oil

5

Dried dill
Dried parsley
Dried paprika
Dried oregano
Chili pepper flakes
Garlic powder
Turmeric
Curry powder
Ground cumin
Ground cinnamon
Extra-virgin olive oil
Sesame oil
Sunflower oil
Sea salt
Whole black peppercorns
Rice or hemp protein powder
Pure vanilla extract

Week 2

Proteins

2 (19-ounce / 540 mL) cans chickpeas
2 (6-ounce / 170 g) cans chunk light tuna
1 (6-ounce / 170 g) can pink sockeye salmon
2 sole fillets
2 halibut fillets
2 tuna steaks
4 boneless, skinless chicken breasts

Whole Grains

2 (3.5-ounce/100 g) packages sesame brown rice crackers
Chickpea flour (about ½ cup/125 mL)
1 (10.5-ounce/300 g) package vermicelli rice noodles
1 (14-ounce/400 g) package Vietnamese rice paper wrappers (8½-inch/22 cm diameter)

Veggies and Fresh Herbs

6 large carrots
1 small red cabbage
4 cups (1 L) Brussels sprouts
1 bunch of kale
1 bunch of red Swiss chard
1 head of cauliflower
1 bunch of asparagus
3 sweet potatoes
1 butternut squash
1 parsnip
1 zucchini
2 red bell peppers
1 orange bell pepper
2 cups (500 mL) sugar snap peas
1 head of Boston Bibb lettuce
1 bunch or bag of fresh spinach

1 English cucumber
1 bunch of celery
2 garlic bulbs
1 bunch of green onions
1 red onion
4 shallots
1 (3-inch/8 cm) piece of fresh gingerroot
2 avocadoes
1 bunch of dill
1 bunch of parsley
1 bunch of oregano
1 bunch of cilantro
1 bunch of thyme
1 bunch of mint
1 (15-ounce/425 g) can artichoke hearts,
   or 1 bag frozen artichoke hearts

Fruits

6 lemons
3 limes
1 fresh pineapple
1 pint (500 mL) fresh blueberries
1 package frozen strawberries
1 (21-ounce/600 g) package
   frozen mixed berries

1 (21-ounce/600 g) package
   frozen açai purée
1 (21-ounce/600 g) package
   frozen blueberries
2 pears
5 apples
3 mangoes

Nuts, Seeds, and Oils

1 cup (250 mL) flaxseeds
½ cup (125 mL) pumpkin seeds
½ cup (125 mL) sesame seeds
1 cup (250 mL) raw walnuts
½ cup (125 mL) pecans
1 cup (250 mL) whole raw almonds

Pantry

Dried thyme
Dried rosemary
Onion powder
Chili powder
Bay leaves
Sunflower oil
Sea salt
Whole black peppercorns
1 (1-quart / 946 mL) box unsweetened rice milk
1 (1-quart / 946 mL) box unsweetened almond milk
Rice or hemp protein powder
Pure vanilla extract

Fourteen-Day Meal Planner

Now that your pantry and fridge are stocked, you have all you need to follow these meal plans using the recipes in this book.

Week 1 Meal Plan

(B = breakfast, L = lunch, SN = snack, and D = dinner.)

Day 1

B: Tropical Twist Smoothie (page 15)
L: Warm Spicy Sweet Potato Salad (page 25)
SN: Basic Hummus (page 86) and rice cakes
D: Easy Roast Chicken (page 38) and brown rice*

Day 2

B: Apples and Cinnamon Brown Rice (page 18)
L: Adzuki Bean and Squash Sauté** (page 53)
SN: Basic Hummus (page 86) and carrot sticks
D: Simple Salmon (page 44) and Sesame Stir-Fry (page 59)

Day 3

B: Tropical Twist Smoothie (page 15)
L: Leftover Easy Roast Chicken (page 38) and Sesame Stir-Fry (page 59)
SN: Apple and almond butter
D: Pesto Rainbow Trout (page 44), Crunchy Broccoli (page 75), and Roasted Beets (page 78)

Day 4

B: Blue Pineapple Smoothie (page 16)
L: Leftover Adzuki Bean and Squash Sauté (page 53)
SN: Guacamole (page 86) and rice crackers
D: Jalapeño-Stuffed Chicken (page 39) and romaine salad with diced cucumbers, shredded carrots, and Tahini-Lemon Dressing (page 84)

Day 5

B: Sweet Quinoa Porridge (page 17)
L: Flax Baked Chicken (page 41) with Roasted Beets and Spinach Salad (page 27)
SN: Basic Hummus (page 86) and cucumber sticks
D: Spring-Green Tuna Pasta (page 48)

Day 6   B: Sweet Quinoa Porridge (page 17)
                 L: Leftover Spring-Green Tuna Pasta (page 48)
                 SN: Handful of walnuts and a pear
                 D: Curried Lentil Stew (page 60) on brown rice*

Day 7   B: Ginger-Pear Amaranth Porridge (page 18)
                 L: Leftover Curried Lentil Stew (page 60)
                 SN: Rice cakes and almond butter
                 D: Kale Rolls (page 57) and Oven-Roasted Squash (page 76)

Week 2 Meal Plan

Day 8   B: Açai Love Smoothie (page 16)
                 L: Leftover Kale Rolls (page 57) and Oven-Roasted Squash (page 76)
                 SN: Apple and almond butter
                 D: Blackened Whitefish (page 48) and Pecan Brussels Sprouts (page 72)

Day 9:   B: Green Goddess Smoothie (page 17)
                 L: Tuna and Salmon Salad (page 29) on spinach leaves
                 SN: Basic Hummus (page 86) and rice crackers
                 D: Crunchy Chicken Nuggets (page 41), Sweet Potato Fries (page 77),
                    and steamed asparagus

Day 10   B: Ginger-Pear Amaranth Porridge (page 18)
                 L: Chickpea Slaw (page 22) and leftover Tuna
                    and Salmon Salad (page 29)
                 SN: Basic Hummus (page 86) and cucumber sticks
                 D: Lemon and Artichoke Halibut (page 47) and Braised
                    Cauliflower (page 80)

Day 11   B: Ginger-Pear Amaranth Porridge (page 18)
          L: Leftover Chickpea Slaw (page 22)
          SN: Apple and almonds
          D: Fresh Salad Rolls (page 54) with Tangy Almond Dipping
              Sauce (page 89)

Day 12   B: Tropical Twist Smoothie (page 15)
          L: Squash Soup (page 33) and leftover Fresh Salad Rolls
              (page 54)
          SN: Rice cakes and almond butter
          D: Vegetable Fritters (page 72), steamed Swiss chard, and
              brown rice* with leftover Tangy Almond Dipping Sauce (page 89)

Day 13   B: Berry-Almond Slam Smoothie (page 15)
          L: Squash Soup (page 33) and leftover Vegetable Fritters (page 72)
          SN: Fresh blueberries and walnuts
          D: Almond Chicken (page 40) on spinach leaves
              with Avocado Dressing (page 84)

Day 14   B: Blue Pineapple Smoothie (page 16)
          L: Tuna-Mango Rolls (page 49)
          SN: Carrot sticks and almond butter
          D: Sesame Tuna (page 45) and Sugar Snap Peas with Ginger
              and Garlic (page 75)

*See Appendix 1, "How to Cook Whole Grains"
**See Appendix 2, "How to Cook Dried Beans"

Top Left: Açai Love Smoothie (page 16)
Top Right: Blueberry Buckwheat Pancakes (page 19)
Bottom: Sweet Quinoa Porridge (page 17)

Breakfasts

Tropical Twist Smoothie

Berry-Almond Slam Smoothie

Açai Love Smoothie

Blue Pineapple Smoothie

Green Goddess Smoothie

Sweet Quinoa Porridge

Ginger-Pear Amaranth Porridge

Apples and Cinnamon Brown Rice

Blueberry Buckwheat Pancakes

Smoothies

Smoothies are super easy and quick to make, whether for a breakfast-to-go or for a leisurely meal at the kitchen table while reading the morning newspaper.

The following five smoothie recipes call for a serving of protein powder as an ingredient. You can use brown rice protein or hemp protein, or a combination protein powder, such as hemp and pea, or a specific detoxification protein powder. Protein powders come with serving-sized spoons, but you can use an amount that suits your unique protein requirement. If you would like to experiment with smoothies as a meal replacement for breakfast, try adding a healthful fat such as almond butter, ground flaxseed, ground hempseed, or fish oil to help keep you full until lunch.

Tropical Twist Smoothie

Yield: 1 serving

Pineapple contains a natural enzyme substance called bromelain that helps break down foods, which improves digestion. Bromelain has also been shown to have anti-inflammatory and anti-coagulant properties, and it is commonly used as a natural treatment for sports injuries.

- ½ ripe fresh mango, peeled and diced
- ½ cup (125 mL) diced fresh pineapple
- 6 frozen strawberries
- 1½ cups (375 mL) water or rice milk or other milk substitute
- 1 serving protein powder
- 1 tablespoon (15 mL) flaxseed oil or hempseed oil

1. Put all the ingredients in a food processor or blender and pulse until smooth, adding more liquid if necessary.

Berry-Almond Slam Smoothie

Yield: 1 serving

The almond butter in this smoothie makes it an ideal meal replacement. If the almond milk is too sweet for your taste buds, feel free to add water instead.

- 1½ cups (375 mL) frozen mixed berries (strawberries, blueberries, and raspberries)
- 1½ cups (375 mL) almond milk
- 1 tablespoon (15 mL) almond butter
- 1 serving protein powder

1. Put all the ingredients in a food processor or blender and pulse until smooth, adding more liquid if necessary.

Blue Pineapple Smoothie

Yield: 1 serving

Part of the fun is experimenting with different fruits and liquids until you find a combination that you love.

* 1 cup (250 mL) diced fresh pineapple
* ½ cup (125 mL) frozen blueberries
* 1½ cups (375 mL) water, rice milk, or other milk substitute
* 1 tablespoon (15 mL) ground flaxseed or ground hempseed
* 1 serving protein powder

1. Put all the ingredients in a food processor or blender and pulse until smooth, adding more liquid if necessary.

Açai Love Smoothie

Yield: 1 serving

The açai berry is a reddish-purple fruit native to Central and South America and is rich in anthocyanins and flavonoids, both powerful antioxidants. It is usually found in the freezer section of a health food store.

* ½ cup (125 mL) frozen açai purée
* ¼ cup (60 mL) frozen blueberries
* ½ mango, peeled and diced
* 1½ cups (375 mL) water or rice milk or other milk substitute
* 1 tablespoon (15 mL) flaxseed oil
* 1 serving protein powder

1. Put all the ingredients in a food processor or blender and pulse until smooth, adding more liquid if necessary.

Green Goddess Smoothie

Yield: 1 serving

You will hardly notice the dark leafy greens in this antioxidant-filled smoothie!

- 1 cup (250 mL) frozen strawberries
- ½ cup (125 mL) diced fresh pineapple
- 1 leaf of kale
- 1 handful of spinach leaves
- 1 to 2 cups (250 to 500 mL) water, rice milk, or other milk substitute
- 1 serving protein powder
- 1 tablespoon (15 mL) ground flaxseed or flaxseed oil

1. Put all the ingredients in a food processor or blender and pulse until smooth, adding more liquid if necessary.

Sweet Quinoa Porridge

Yield: 2 servings

Rinsing the quinoa is important to avoid a raw or bitter taste. Don't be put off by the soapy bubbles that form while rinsing off the saponin coat.

- ½ cup (125 mL) quinoa
- 1 cup (250 mL) water
- ½ teaspoon (2 mL) cinnamon
- ¼ teaspoon (1 mL) sea salt
- ½ cup (125 mL) unsweetened rice or almond milk
- 1 small apple, peeled and diced
- ½ cup (125 mL) fresh or frozen blueberries
- ¼ cup (60 mL) slivered almonds

1. Rinse the quinoa and drain in a fine sieve.
2. Put the quinoa, water, cinnamon, and salt in a small saucepan and place over high heat. Bring to a boil, uncovered.
3. Reduce the heat to low, cover, and simmer for 15 minutes, until almost all the water is absorbed.
4. Stir in the milk, apple, blueberries, and almonds and simmer, uncovered, for another 10 minutes. Let sit for 5 minutes before serving.

Apples and Cinnamon Brown Rice

Yield: 2 servings

This is a great way to use leftover brown rice and get in your daily dose of the blood-sugar-lowering spice, cinnamon!

- 1 cup (250 mL) cooked brown rice
- 1 cup (250 mL) unsweetened rice or almond milk
- 1 apple, diced
- 2 tablespoons (30 mL) ground flaxseed
- 2 tablespoons (30 mL) slivered almonds
- ½ teaspoon (2 mL) cinnamon
- ⅛ teaspoon (0.5 mL) sea salt

1. Combine all the ingredients in a small saucepan and cook over medium-low heat for 5 minutes, stirring occasionally.

Ginger-Pear Amaranth Porridge

Yield: 2 servings

To save some time in the morning, make enough for a few days, without the walnuts, store in the refrigerator, and then just reheat, adding a touch more rice milk and the walnuts.

- ¾ cup (185 mL) amaranth
- ¼ teaspoon (1 mL) sea salt
- 1¼ cups (310 mL) water
- 1 small pear, diced
- ¼ cup (60 mL) walnut halves
- 1 teaspoon (5 mL) peeled and grated fresh gingerroot
- ¼ teaspoon (1 mL) vanilla extract
- ½ teaspoon (2 mL) cinnamon
- ¼ cup (60 mL) unsweetened rice or almond milk

1. Rinse the amaranth in a saucepan and drain as much water as you can. Using a sieve will not work with this tiny, fine grain.
2. Put the amaranth, salt, and water in a small saucepan and bring to a boil, uncovered, over high heat. This should take about 3 minutes.
3. Reduce the heat to medium-low and simmer, covered, for about 20 minutes, stirring occasionally, until almost all the water is absorbed.
4. Stir in the pear, walnuts, gingerroot, vanilla, cinnamon, and milk and simmer, covered, for another 5 minutes. Let sit for 5 minutes more before serving.

Blueberry Buckwheat Pancakes

Yield: **8** pancakes

Instead of maple syrup, these pancakes can be topped with 1 tablespoon (15 mL) of Roasted Apples (page 90).

- ¾ (180 mL) cups light or dark buckwheat flour
- ½ teaspoon (5 mL) cinnamon
- ¼ teaspoon (1 mL) sea salt
- 1 cup (250 mL) fresh or frozen blueberries
- 3 tablespoons (45 mL) unsweetened rice or almond milk
- 3 tablespoons (45 mL) water
- 2 tablespoons (30 mL) sunflower oil
- ½ teaspoon (2 mL) vanilla extract
- 1 flax egg replacer*

*To make the flax egg replacer, combine 1 tablespoon (15 mL) of ground flaxseed with 3 tablespoons (45 mL) of water and let it sit for 2 minutes.

1. Stir the flour, cinnamon, and salt together in a medium mixing bowl. Stir in the blueberries.
2. Combine the milk, water, 1 tablespoon (15 mL) of the sunflower oil, and the vanilla in a small bowl.
3. Stir the flax egg replacer into the milk mixture.
4. Pour the milk mixture into the flour mixture, mixing until just combined, using a whisk if necessary. If the batter is too stiff, add a little more milk.
5. Heat the remaining 1 tablespoon (15 mL) of sunflower oil on a griddle or in a sauté pan over medium-low heat, and then pour 2 tablespoons (30 mL) of the batter onto the griddle or into the saute pan, making 4 pancakes. Buckwheat flour browns quickly, so make sure the griddle or pan is not too hot.
6. Once the edges are slightly browned and a few bubbles have formed on top, flip the pancakes over to cook the other side.

Salads and Slaws

Top: Asparagus and Fennel Slaw (page 24)

Four-Colour Slaw

Yield: 4 servings

This recipe includes cooked beets. Don't know how to cook beets? Wash and scrub them, cut the tops and bottoms off, and then put them in a saucepan and cover with water. Cover and bring to a boil over high heat, and then reduce the heat to medium and cook for 40 minutes, or until the beets are easily pierced with a fork.

- 3 tablespoons (45 mL) pumpkin seeds
- 3 tablespoons (45 mL) sunflower seeds
- 3 medium carrots, peeled and shredded
- ¼ head of green or red cabbage, shredded
- 2 tablespoons (30 mL) minced fresh parsley
- 2 tablespoons (30 mL) snipped fresh dill
- 4 medium cooked and cooled beets, peeled and shredded
- 6 tablespoons (90 mL) sunflower oil
- Juice of half a lemon
- Zest of half a lemon
- ½ teaspooon (2 mL) sea salt
- ½ teaspoon (2 mL) freshly ground pepper

1. Heat a sauté pan over medium heat and then add the pumpkin and sunflower seeds, stirring constantly until lightly toasted, about 3 minutes. Set aside to cool.
2. Combine the carrots, cabbage, parsley, dill, and toasted seeds in a serving bowl. Top with the shredded beets.
3. Whisk together the sunflower oil, lemon juice and zest, salt, and pepper in a small bowl, and then pour over the salad, tossing to coat evenly.

Chickpea Slaw

Yield: 4 servings

A food processor to shred the carrots, kale, and cabbage will cut the prep time for this recipe to less than 10 minutes. If you don't have chickpeas, feel free to substitute them with any protein. You could add a different bean or a can of tuna or some grilled chicken breast.

- 2 medium carrots, peeled and shredded
- 1 small bunch of kale, shredded
- ½ small head of red cabbage, shredded
- 1 (19-ounce / 540 mL) can chickpeas, drained and rinsed
- 2 tablespoons (30 mL) pumpkin seeds
- 1 teaspoon (5 mL) dried dill, or 1 tablespoon (15 mL) snipped fresh dill
- 1 teaspoon (5 mL) dried oregano, or 1 tablespoon (15 mL) chopped fresh oregano
- ½ teaspoon (2 mL) sea salt
- ½ teaspoon (2 mL) freshly ground pepper
- ½ teaspoon (2 mL) chili pepper flakes
- ½ cup (125 mL) extra-virgin olive oil
- Juice of 1 lemon

1. Mix the carrots, kale, cabbage, chickpeas, and pumpkin seeds in a serving bowl and set aside.
2. To make the dressing, combine the dill, oregano, salt, chili pepper flakes, and pepper in a small bowl, and then add the olive oil and lemon juice and whisk until well blended. Pour the dressing over the slaw, tossing to coat evenly.

Bottom: Warm Spicy Sweet Potato Salad (page 25)

Asparagus and Fennel Slaw

Yield: 4 servings

Fennel is a crunchy and slightly sweet vegetable that can be eaten cooked or raw and is helpful for indigestion. It is common practice in India to chew on fennel seeds after dinner to help digestion and keep bad breath away.

- 1 bunch of thin asparagus
- Juice of 1 lemon
- ¼ cup (60 mL) extra-virgin olive oil
- ½ teaspoon (2 mL) sea salt
- 1 teaspoon (5 mL) freshly ground pepper
- ½ teaspoon (2 mL) fennel seeds
- 2 tablespoons (30 mL) chopped fresh mint
- 1 large fennel bulb, thinly sliced
- 1 red bell pepper, seeded and thinly sliced
- ½ small red onion, thinly sliced

1. Bring a medium saucepan of water to a boil over high heat.
2. Break off the bottom tough ends of the asparagus, put them in the saucepan, and boil for 2 minutes.
3. Drain the asparagus and immediately rinse under cold running water until cool and drain again. Cut into 2-inch pieces and place in a large serving bowl.
4. To make the dressing, whisk together the lemon juice, olive oil, salt, pepper, fennel seeds, and mint in a small bowl.
5. Add the fennel slices, bell pepper, and onion to the asparagus, pour the dressing over top, and toss to coat evenly.

Quinoa Tabbouleh

Yield: 4 servings

To make a full meal for four people, double the quinoa and water and add diced chicken breast, tuna, or chickpeas.

- 1 cup (250 mL) quinoa
- 2 cups (500 mL) water
- ½ English cucumber, diced
- 4 celery stalks, diced
- ½ small red onion, minced
- 2 cups (500 mL) loosely packed, minced fresh parsley
- 3 tablespoons (45 mL) minced fresh cilantro
- ⅓ cup (80 mL) extra-virgin olive oil
- Juice of 1 lemon
- 1 teaspoon (5 mL) sea salt
- 1 teaspoon (5 mL) freshly ground pepper

1. Wash the quinoa thoroughly to remove any trace of the bitter white coating, then rinse and drain.
2. Bring the water to a boil in a medium-sized saucepan. Add the quinoa and reduce the heat to low, cover, and simmer until all the water is absorbed, about 20 minutes.
3. Place the quinoa in a large serving bowl and set aside to cool and dry completely. Add the cucumber, celery, onion, parsley, and cilantro.
4. To make the dressing, whisk together the olive oil, lemon juice, salt, and pepper in a small bowl. Pour the dressing over the salad and toss well to combine.
5. Cover and refrigerate for at least 1 hour before serving. Serve chilled.

Warm Spicy Sweet Potato Salad

Yield: 4 servings

This recipe includes adzuki beans, which are small, reddish-brown beans that have a sweet and nutty flavour, are a great source of folate and iron, and can be found in most bulk stores. Black beans can be substituted for adzuki beans if necessary. One 15-ounce (425 g) can is equivalent to 1½ cups (375 mL) of cooked beans, which is ⅔ cup (160 mL) of dried beans.

- 2 medium sweet potatoes, diced
- 1 small red onion, diced
- 1 tablespoon (15 mL) plus ¼ cup (60 mL) extra-virgin olive oil
- 1 cup loosely packed, chopped fresh cilantro
- 1 (15-ounce / 500 g) can adzuki beans, drained and rinsed
- 1 yellow bell pepper, seeded and diced
- 1 garlic clove, coarsely chopped
- 1 jalapeño pepper, seeded
- Juice of 1 lime
- ½ teaspoon (2 mL) sea salt
- ½ teaspoon (2 mL) freshly ground pepper

1. Preheat the oven to 450°F (230°C).
2. Place the sweet potatoes and onion on a baking sheet and drizzle with the 1 tablespoon (15 mL) of olive oil to coat. Roast in the oven for 25 minutes.
3. While the sweet potatoes are roasting, toss the cilantro, beans, and bell pepper in a small bowl.
4. To make the dressing, combine the garlic, jalapeño pepper, lime, salt, and pepper in a small food chopper or processor. Process for 10 seconds, and then add the ¼ cup (60 mL) of olive oil and continue to process for another minute.
5. Toss the roasted sweet potatoes and onion with the bean mixture and pour the dressing over top. Combine to thoroughly coat and serve warm.

Mango and Mung Bean Salad

Yield: 4 servings

Mung beans are small green beans that are easy to digest. Like most beans, they are high in soluble fibre, decreasing the risk of heart disease and diabetes.

- 1½ cups (375 mL) mung beans
- 3 cups (750 mL) water
- 1 large carrot, peeled and shredded
- 1 firm ripe mango, peeled and julienned
- 1 small Granny Smith apple, julienned
- ½ red bell pepper, seeded and julienned
- 1 teaspoon (5 mL) peeled and grated fresh gingerroot
- ½ teaspoon (2 mL) sea salt
- Juice of 1 lemon
- Zest of 1 lemon
- 1 tablespoon (15 mL) sunflower oil
- ½ teaspoon (2 mL) black mustard seeds
- 1 small jalapeño pepper, seeded and minced
- 1 tablespoon (15 mL) chopped fresh cilantro

1. Soak the mung beans in the water for 12 hours.
2. Drain the mung beans and place in a large serving bowl with the carrot, mango, apple, bell pepper, ginger, salt, and lemon juice and zest.
3. Heat the sunflower oil in a small sauté pan over medium heat. Add the mustard seeds and cook until the seeds start popping.
4. Add the jalapeño pepper to the mustard seeds and stir for 1 minute.
5. Add the jalapeño pepper, mustard seeds, and the cilantro to the bean mixture and toss to combine.

Lentil Salad

Yield: 4 servings

French lentils, also called Puy lentils from the name of the capital of the Velay region in France, where they originated, are delicate and peppery legumes that retain their shape with cooking.

- 1 cup (250 mL) dried French lentils
- 2½ cups (625 mL) water
- ¼ cup (60 mL) extra-virgin olive oil
- Juice of 1 large lemon
- 2 teaspoons (10 mL) dried basil
- 1½ teaspoons (7 mL) sea salt
- 1 teaspoon (5 mL) freshly ground pepper
- 1 teaspoon (5 mL) chili pepper flakes
- 1 cup (250 mL) minced fresh parsley
- 2 garlic cloves, minced
- 4 green onions, thinly sliced
- 1 red bell pepper, seeded and thinly sliced
- 1 yellow bell pepper, seeded and thinly sliced

1. Wash the lentils by covering them with cold water and picking out any pebbles or floating particles. Rinse and drain.
2. Put the water in a large saucepan and bring to a boil. Add the lentils, reduce the heat to low, and cover and cook for 20 minutes, or until tender.
3. Remove the lentils from the heat, drain, and rinse under cold water to cool. Drain again and place in a large bowl.
4. To make the dressing, put the olive oil, lemon juice, basil, salt, pepper, and chili flakes in a small bowl and mix well.
5. Add the parsley, garlic, green onions, and bell peppers to the lentils and pour the dressing over top, tossing to coat evenly.

Roasted Beets and Spinach Salad

Yield: 2 servings

The walnuts in this salad are a great source of omega-3 fatty acids, a healthful protective fat the body cannot make on its own. Adding walnuts to your diet can improve your cardiovascular health, cognitive function, and inflammatory skin problems, such as eczema.

- 6 small beets, boiled and quartered
- 1 fennel bulb, tops cut off and bulb quartered
- 2 tablespoons (30 mL) plus ¼ cup (60 mL) extra-virgin olive oil
- 4 cups (1 L) loosely packed baby spinach leaves
- 1 small avocado, peeled and diced
- 1 small shallot, minced
- Juice of half a lemon
- ½ teaspoon (2 mL) sea salt
- ½ teaspoon (2 mL) freshly ground pepper
- ½ cup (125 mL) walnut halves, toasted

1. Preheat the oven to 450°F (230°C).
2. Place the beets and fennel on a baking sheet, drizzle the 2 tablespoons (30 mL) of olive oil over top, and roast in the oven for 15 minutes.
3. Meanwhile, combine the spinach and avocado in a mixing bowl.
4. To make the dressing, put the shallot, lemon juice, salt, pepper, and the ¼ cup (60 mL) of olive oil in a small food processor and pulse for 1 minute.
5. Toss the dressing with the spinach and avocado and place on two serving plates.
6. Place half the roasted beets and fennel on each plate and sprinkle the walnuts over each serving.

Tuna and Salmon Salad

Yield: 4 servings

Most people are used to making tuna with mayonnaise. This recipe proves that tuna salad can be clean and healthful. The mixture can be eaten on top of a salad, as a snack with rice crackers, or with raw veggies.

- 1 (6-ounce / 170 g) can chunk white tuna, drained and rinsed
- 1 (6-ounce / 170 g) can red sockeye salmon, drained and rinsed, skin removed
- 4 celery stalks, finely diced
- ½ English cucumber, finely diced
- ¼ cup (60 mL) extra-virgin olive oil
- Juice of half a lemon
- ¼ cup (60 mL) loosely packed, snipped fresh dill, or 4 teaspoons (20 mL) dried dill
- ½ teaspoon (2 mL) sea salt
- ½ teaspoon (2 mL) freshly ground pepper

1. Place the tuna and salmon in a small bowl and mash with a fork until well blended.
2. Add the remaining ingredients and mix thoroughly.

Thai Carrot Soup (page 32)

Soups

Thai Carrot Soup

Yield: 4 servings

If you are lucky enough to find fresh lemongrass stalks at your grocery store, substitute the lemongrass purée for three stalks. Cut off and discard the hard top ends, hard outer leaves, and roots and bruise the stalks with the flat side of a large, heavy knife or a meat pounder before adding to the stockpot.

- 3 tablespoons (45 mL) sunflower oil
- 2 tablespoons (30 mL) lemongrass purée*
- 3 tablespoons (45 mL) peeled and sliced fresh gingerroot
- 2 garlic cloves, minced
- 6 tablespoons raw, unsalted cashews
- 8 large carrots, cut into 1-inch pieces
- 1 teaspoon (5 mL) sea salt
- ¼ teaspoon (1 mL) cayenne
- 1 (32-ounce / 946 mL) box rice milk
- 2 cups (500 mL) water
- ½ cup (125 mL) loosely packed, chopped fresh cilantro leaves
- Juice of 1 lime

*Available in Asian grocery stores and many supermarkets

1. Heat the sunflower oil in a large stockpot over medium heat, and when hot, add the lemongrass, gingerroot, cashews, and garlic.
2. Cook, stirring frequently, until the garlic is golden, watching carefully not to burn the garlic, about 5 minutes.
3. Add the carrots, salt, and cayenne and cook for 1 minute, and then add the rice milk and water. Reduce the heat to low and stir in ¼ cup (60 mL) of the cilantro, cover, and simmer for 30 minutes, or until the carrots are tender.
4. Purée the soup in batches in a food processor or blender, or use an immersion hand blender.
5. Add the lime juice and garnish with the remaining ¼ cup (60 mL) of the cilantro before serving.

Puréed Mung Bean Soup

Yield: 8 to 10 cups

Kale may not tickle everyone's taste buds when eaten on its own. However, putting it in soups and stews is a great way to reduce the bitter taste and still increase the nutritional quality of the dish.

- 1 cup (250 mL) mung beans
- 3 tablespoons (45 mL) extra-virgin olive oil
- 1 medium yellow onion, diced
- 2 leeks, white and green parts, sliced
- 3 celery stalks, diced
- 4 garlic cloves, minced
- 1 teaspoon (5 mL) dried oregano
- 1 teaspoon (5 mL) dried savory
- ½ teaspoon (2 mL) dried rosemary
- ½ teaspoon (2 mL) dried thyme
- 1 teaspoon (5 mL) sea salt
- 1 teaspoon (5 mL) freshly ground pepper
- 2 large carrots, diced
- 1 large sweet potato, diced
- 2 to 3 bay leaves
- 8 cups (2 L) water
- 1 small bunch of kale, coarsely chopped and coarse stems removed
- Juice of 1 lemon
- 1 cup (250 mL) coarsely chopped fresh parsley

1. Soak the beans in water for 3 hours. Drain and set aside.
2. Heat the olive oil in a large stockpot over medium heat. Add the onion, leeks, celery, garlic, and the oregano, savory, rosemary, thyme, salt, and pepper.
3. Cook, stirring occasionally, for 10 minutes.
4. Add the carrots, sweet potatoes, mung beans, bay leaves, and water. Cover and simmer over low heat for 20 minutes, until the vegetables are tender.
5. Add the kale, and simmer for another 10 minutes, or until the kale wilts.
6. Remove the pot from the stove and add the lemon juice and parsley. Stir through and let cool for 5 minutes.
7. Purée in batches in a food processor or blender, or use an immersion hand blender.

Lentil Soup

Yield: 8 cups

Making this soup when time permits and freezing it in individual containers can be a lifesaver when it comes to a detox. Nothing is better than coming home after a hard day of work and having something healthful and ready to reheat in less than 5 minutes!

- 2 tablespoons (30 mL) extra-virgin olive oil
- ½ teaspoon (2 mL) chili pepper flakes
- 1 large yellow onion, diced
- 2 garlic cloves, minced
- 3 large carrots, diced
- 2 celery stalks, diced
- 2 large parsnips, diced
- 1 cup (250 mL) lentils
- 2 sweet potatoes, diced
- 6 cups (1.5 L) vegetable or chicken stock
- ½ cup (125 mL) chopped fresh parsley, or 1 tablespoon (15 mL) dried parsley
- ½ cup (125 mL) chopped fresh thyme, or 1 tablespoon (15 mL) dried thyme
- ½ teaspoon (2 mL) cumin seeds
- 1 teaspoon (5 mL) sea salt
- 1 teaspoon (5 mL) freshly ground pepper

1. Heat the olive oil in a large stockpot over medium heat. Add the chili pepper flakes, onion, garlic, carrots, and celery. Stir occasionally for 10 minutes until the vegetables are tender.
2. Add the parsnips and cook, stirring, for an additional 5 minutes.
3. Add the lentils and sweet potatoes and 1 cup (250 mL) of the stock and cook for 10 minutes.
4. Add the rest of the stock, parsley, thyme, cumin, salt, and pepper. Cover and simmer over low heat for about 45 minutes, or until the vegetables are tender.
5. At this time, you can leave the soup as is or, using a food processor, blender, or immersion hand blender, purée until smooth.

Squash Soup

Yield: 6 to 8 cups

Did you know that butternut squash is technically a fruit because it contains seeds? The rich orange colour of the flesh signals its content of beta-carotene, which is protective against heart disease and macular degeneration.

- 2 tablespoons (30 mL) extra-virgin olive oil
- 2 small yellow onions, diced
- 3 garlic cloves, minced
- 2 large carrots, peeled and diced
- 1 large parsnip, peeled and diced
- 2 celery stalks, coarsely chopped
- 1 large butternut squash, peeled, seeds removed, and diced
- 6 cups (1.5 L) water
- ½ cup (250 mL) loosely packed, finely chopped fresh parsley
- 5 sprigs of fresh thyme, finely chopped
- 1 tablespoon (15 mL) peeled and grated fresh gingerroot
- 2 bay leaves
- 1 teaspoon (5 mL) sea salt
- 1 teaspoon (5 mL) freshly ground pepper
- Juice of half a lemon

1. Heat the olive oil in a large stockpot over medium heat. Add the onions and garlic and cook, stirring occasionally, watching that the garlic does not burn, about 10 minutes.
2. Add the carrots, parsnips, celery, and squash and cook, stirring, for another 2 minutes.
3. Add the water, parsley, thyme, gingerroot, bay leaves, salt, and pepper. Cover and bring to a boil over medium-high heat, and then reduce the heat to low.
4. Let simmer until the vegetables are tender, about 45 minutes.
5. Remove from the heat and let cool for 15 minutes.
6. Purée the soup in batches in a food processor or blender, or use an immersion hand blender, until the soup is smooth.
7. Add the lemon juice and stir through.

Basic Vegetable Stock

Yield: 8 to 10 cups

Frozen homemade stock is nice to have around to flavour an everyday quinoa or brown rice. Make sure to cool the stock completely before freezing. Another helpful tip is to measure out 2 cups (500 mL) of stock in each container so there is no guessing as to quantity when defrosting for use.

- 3 large carrots, unpeeled, washed, and coarsely chopped
- 3 large parsnips, unpeeled, washed, and coarsely chopped
- 3 celery stalks, with leaves, coarsely chopped
- 3 small yellow onions, unpeeled, washed, and quartered
- 1 whole garlic bulb, unpeeled and smashed
- 4 sprigs of fresh thyme
- ½ cup (125 mL) chopped fresh parsley
- ½ teaspoon (2 mL) sea salt
- 3 bay leaves
- 10 whole black peppercorns
- 8 to 10 cups (2 to 2.5 L) water

1. Put all the ingredients in a large stockpot and cover with cold water.
2. Cover the pot and bring to a boil over high heat. Reduce the heat to low and simmer for 1 hour.
3. Remove from the heat and let cool for 15 minutes.
4. Using a colander, strain the liquid to use the stock immediately, or allow to cool completely, and then freeze in 2-cup (500 mL) portions.

Mains
Chicken

Easy Roast Chicken

Jalapeño-Stuffed Chicken

Sesame-Lime Chicken

Almond Chicken

Flax Baked Chicken

Crunchy Chicken Nuggets

Top: Easy Roast Chicken (page 38)
Bottom: Easy Roast Chicken with Beet Greens (page 73)

Easy Roast Chicken

Yield: 4 servings

Reserve the leftover chicken carcass and vegetables from this recipe to make a delicious chicken stock. Put everything in a large stockpot, cover with water, and bring to a boil. Reduce the heat and let the stock simmer, covered, for 2 hours. Cool and put in the refrigerator overnight. In the morning, skim off the fat and pour the stock into glass jars in 2-cup portions and freeze for later use. This is another helpful step that is great to do on your first prep day in order to have lots of detox-friendly chicken stock on hand.

- 1 large yellow onion, coarsely chopped
- 3 large carrots, coarsely chopped
- 3 celery stalks, coarsely chopped
- 1 fennel bulb, including top stalks, coarsely chopped
- 6 tablespoons (90 mL) extra-virgin olive oil
- 2 teaspoons (10 mL) sea salt
- 2 teaspoons (10 mL) freshly ground pepper
- 1 (5-pound / 2.2 kg) roasting chicken
- 1 large bunch of fresh thyme
- 1 lemon, halved
- 1 whole garlic bulb, halved

1. Preheat the oven to 425°F (220°C).
2. Place the onion, carrots, celery, and fennel in a large roasting pan.
3. Add 3 tablespoons (45 mL) of the olive oil, ½ teaspoon (2 mL) of the salt, ½ teaspoon (2 mL) of the pepper, and half the bunch of thyme to the vegetables and toss to coat.
4. Rinse the chicken inside and out and pat dry with paper towels, and then place it on top of the vegetables in the roasting pan.
5. Sprinkle ½ teaspoon (2 mL) of the salt and ½ teaspoon (2 mL) of the pepper inside the chicken.
6. Place the lemon and garlic bulb halves and the remaining half bunch of thyme inside the chicken.
7. Sprinkle the remaining 1 teaspoon (5 mL) of the salt and the remaining 1 teaspoon (5 mL) of the pepper on the outside of the chicken and drizzle with the remaining 3 tablespoons (45 mL) of olive oil to coat.
8. Place the chicken in the oven and roast for 90 minutes, checking at 75 minutes. The chicken is done when the juices run clear when a leg is cut or pulled away.
9. Remove from the oven, cover with aluminum foil, and let rest for 20 minutes before serving.

Jalapeño-Stuffed Chicken

Yield: 2 servings

The pumpkin seeds in this recipe are a great source of zinc, an important mineral for immune function and the prostate. Pumpkin seeds are also a natural anti-inflammatory and may help prevent kidney stone formation.

- 3 tablespoons (45 mL) pumpkin seeds
- ¼ cup (60 mL) extra-virgin olive oil
- 1 jalapeño pepper, seeded and chopped
- 2 garlic cloves, minced
- 1½ teaspoons (7 mL) sea salt
- ¼ cup (60 mL) brown rice flour
- 1 teaspoon (5 mL) freshly ground pepper
- 2 boneless, skinless chicken breasts

1. Heat a medium-sized sauté pan over low heat, add the pumpkin seeds, and toast, stirring frequently, for 3 minutes.
2. Remove the pan from the heat and put the toasted pumpkin seeds in small food chopper or processor.
3. Heat the olive oil in the same sauté pan over medium-low heat for 1 minute, and then add the jalapeño pepper and garlic and stir through for a few minutes, watching that the garlic doesn't burn.
4. Remove the pan from the heat and put the jalapeño mixture, with the olive oil, in the food chopper with the pumpkin seeds. Process for 5 seconds, and then add ½ teaspoon (2 mL) of the salt.
5. Mix the flour, the remaining 1 teaspoon (5 mL) of salt, and the pepper in a mixing bowl.
6. Make a slit lengthwise along the side of each chicken breast to make a pocket.
7. Place half the jalapeño mixture in each pocket, and then coat each side of the chicken breasts with the flour mixture.
8. Place the chicken breasts in a heated sauté pan and cook over medium heat for 5 minutes. Flip the breasts over to cook the other the side for another 3 minutes.
9. Cover, turn off the heat, and let the chicken sit in the sauté pan for another 5 minutes before serving.

Sesame-Lime Chicken

Yield: 2 servings

Ginger, an ingredient in this dish, is a warming herb and is known for its powers to help nausea. It is also a powerful anti-inflammatory herb and can help knock out a fever!

- Juice of 1 lime
- 1 tablespoon (15 mL) ground cumin
- 2 garlic cloves, minced
- 2 tablespoons (30 mL) peeled and minced fresh gingerroot
- 2 tablespoons (30 mL) sesame seeds
- ½ teaspoon (2 mL) sea salt
- 1 teaspoon (5 mL) freshly ground pepper
- 2 boneless, skinless chicken breasts
- 2 tablespoons (30 mL) sunflower oil

1. Reserve a little of the lime juice for drizzling later, and combine the rest with the cumin, garlic, gingerroot, sesame seeds, salt, and pepper in a shallow bowl.
2. Rinse the chicken breasts and pat dry with paper towels and place in the bowl with the lime mixture. Turn to coat thoroughly.
3. Place the chicken in the refrigerator and let sit for at least 1 hour or overnight.
4. Heat the olive oil in a sauté pan over medium-high heat, add the chicken breasts and the marinade, and cook for 3 minutes, and then flip them over and cook for another 3 minutes to nicely brown both sides.
5. Reduce the heat to medium-low and cover and continue to cook for 5 minutes more, and then turn off the heat and let the chicken sit in the pan for another 2 minutes.
6. Drizzle the reserved lime juice over the chicken and serve.

Almond Chicken

Yield: 2 servings

A high-fat food that is good for you? Almonds are high in monounsaturated fats, the same type of fats found in olive oil. People who eat nuts at least twice per week are less likely to gain weight than those who almost never eat nuts!

- ½ cup (125 mL) ground almonds
- 1 tablespoon (15 mL) dried oregano
- 1 tablespoon (15 mL) dried basil
- 1 tablespoon (15 mL) dried parsley
- ½ teaspoon (2 mL) sea salt
- 1 teaspoon (5 mL) freshly ground pepper
- 2 tablespoons (30 mL) extra-virgin olive oil
- 2 boneless, skinless chicken breasts

1. Preheat the oven to 450°F (230°C).
2. Combine the almonds, oregano, basil, parsley, salt, and pepper in a small bowl.
3. Rinse the chicken breasts and pat dry with paper towels and place on a plate.
4. Gently pat the chicken on each side with the almond mixture and place on a baking sheet or in a shallow glass baking dish.
5. Drizzle the olive oil over the chicken and bake in the oven for 12 to 15 minutes, depending on the thickness of each breast.

Flax Baked Chicken

Yield: 2 servings

Any gluten-free flour will do in this recipe. Flours other than brown rice flour to consider are quinoa, buckwheat, millet, or chickpea.

- 2 tablespoons (30 mL) brown rice flour
- 1 tablespoon (15 mL) ground flaxseed
- 1 teaspoon (5 mL) dried parsley
- 1 teaspoon (5 mL) dried paprika
- 1 teaspoon (5 mL) garlic powder
- ½ teaspoon (2 mL) turmeric
- ½ teaspoon (2 mL) sea salt
- 1 teaspoon (5 mL) freshly ground pepper
- 2 boneless, skinless chicken breasts
- 3 tablespoons (45 mL) extra-virgin olive oil

1. Preheat the oven to 450°F (230°C).
2. In a small mixing bowl, combine the flour, flaxseed, parsley, paprika, garlic powder, turmeric, salt, and pepper.
3. Place the flour mixture in a Ziploc bag.
4. Rinse and pat the chicken breasts dry. Coat the breasts with the olive oil.
5. Put the chicken in the bag with the flour mixture and thoroughly coat each piece.
6. Place the chicken on a baking sheet or shallow glass baking dish and bake in the oven for 12 to 15 minutes, depending on thickness of the chicken.

Crunchy Chicken Nuggets

Yield: 2 servings

Using scissors to cut the chicken breasts into nugget-sized pieces is an easy way to make this healthful fast food.

- ¼ cup (60 mL) brown rice flour
- 20 sesame brown rice crackers
- 1 teaspoon (5 mL) dried parsley
- 1 teaspoon (5 mL) garlic powder
- ½ teaspoon (2 mL) onion powder
- ½ teaspoon (2 mL) sea salt
- ½ teaspoon (2 mL) freshly ground pepper
- 2 boneless, skinless chicken breasts
- ¼ cup (60 mL) extra-virgin olive oil

1. Preheat the oven to 450°F (230°C).
2. In a food processor or blender, combine the flour, rice crackers, parsley, garlic powder, onion powder, salt, and pepper and pulse until the mixture looks like coarse bread crumbs.
3. Put the flour mixture in a large Ziploc bag.
4. Rinse and pat the chicken breasts dry, and cut into nugget-sized pieces.
5. Coat the nuggets with the olive oil, and then place the pieces in the bag with the flour mixture and coat thoroughly.
6. Place the nuggets on a baking sheet or shallow glass baking dish and bake in the oven for 12 to 15 minutes, depending on the thickness of the chicken.

Mains

Fish

Simple Salmon

Pesto Rainbow Trout

Sesame Tuna

Pan-Fried Sole

Lemon and Artichoke Halibut

Blackened Whitefish

Spring-Green Tuna Pasta

Tuna-Mango Rolls

Pesto Rainbow Trout

Yield: 2 servings

When selecting fish, try to find fillets that are of even thickness. This helps to cook fish uniformly. If the ends of the fillets are thinner, fold them under when placing the fish on a baking sheet.

- 1 large rainbow trout fillet
- 2 tablespoons (30 mL) Parsley Pesto (page 88)
- 1 tablespoon (15 mL) extra-virgin olive oil

1. Preheat the oven broiler to high-broil.
2. Spread the parsley pesto over the trout fillet and place it on a baking sheet.
3. Drizzle the fish with the olive oil and place it under the broiler.
4. Broil for 5 minutes, or until the fish flakes with a fork.

Simple Salmon

Yield: 2 servings

This is the easiest and healthiest recipe in the book! The omega-3 fatty acids in salmon may help prevent heart disease and stroke by lowering the body's rate of blood clotting. Salmon may also lower LDL cholesterol and can help stabilize blood sugar levels.

- 2 salmon steaks or salmon fillets, about 1 inch (2.5 cm) thick
- ½ teaspoon (2 mL) sea salt
- 1 teaspoon (5 mL) freshly ground pepper
- 2 teaspoons (10 mL) dried dill, or 2 tablespoons (30 mL) snipped fresh dill
- 2 tablespoons (30 mL) extra-virgin olive oil

1. Preheat the oven broiler to high-broil.
2. Rinse and pat dry the salmon fillets and place them on a baking sheet.
3. Sprinkle the fillets evenly with the salt, pepper, and dill.
4. Drizzle the olive oil over the salmon and place under the broiler for 5 minutes, longer if the fillets are thicker than 1 inch (2.5 cm).
5. After 5 minutes, shut off the broiler, but let the salmon sit in the oven for 1 more minute, and then remove it from the oven and let sit for 1 minute longer before serving.

44

Sesame Tuna

Yield: 2 servings

When buying tuna, look at the colour of the flesh. It should be pink or red without any hint of browning. To get the best out of your tuna, make sure not to overcook it. It should still be moist inside and the flesh will be opaque after cooking.

- Juice of half a lime
- 2 (1-inch / 2.5 cm) thick tuna steaks
- ½ teaspoon (2 mL) sea salt
- 1 teaspoon (5 mL) freshly ground pepper
- 2 tablespoons (30 mL) sesame oil
- 4 tablespoons (60 mL) sesame seeds

1. Preheat the oven broiler to high-broil.
2. Squeeze the lime juice over both sides of the tuna steaks.
3. Season the steaks with the salt and pepper and sprinkle the sesame oil evenly over both sides.
4. Pat the sesame seeds evenly on both sides of the tuna steaks and place them on a baking sheet. Let sit for 15 minutes, and then place under the broiler.
5. Broil the steaks for 2 minutes, and then flip them over and broil the other side for 2 minutes.

Pan-Fried Sole

Yield: 2 servings

Served with Sweet Potato Fries (page 77), this recipe could be a detox-friendly version of fish and chips!

- 2 sole fillets
- ¼ cup (60 mL) rice milk
- ½ cup (125 mL) brown rice flour
- 1 tablespoon (15 mL) finely minced fresh parsley
- 1 teaspoon (5 mL) paprika
- ½ teaspoon (2 mL) sea salt
- 1 teaspoon (5 mL) freshly ground pepper
- Zest of 1 lemon
- 2 tablespoons (30 mL) extra-virgin olive oil or sunflower oil
- Juice of 1 lemon

1. Rinse the sole fillets and pat dry with paper towels.
2. Place the sole on a plate and pour the rice milk over top. Let soak for 5 minutes.
3. Meanwhile, combine the flour, parsley, paprika, salt, pepper, and lemon zest in a deep pie plate.
4. Take each sole fillet out of the rice milk and place in the flour mixture. Flip the sole over to make sure both sides of are well covered with flour.
5. Heat the olive oil over medium heat in a medium sauté pan for a few minutes. Place the sole fillets in the pan and cook each side for 3 minutes. Drizzle the lemon juice over the fish before serving.

Lemon and Artichoke Halibut

Yield: 2 servings

The artichoke is a vegetable that contains a powerful compound called cynarin that improves liver and gallbladder function, and lowers cholesterol.

- 4 tablespoons (60 mL) extra-virgin olive oil
- 2 halibut fillets
- 1 teaspoon (5 mL) sea salt
- 1½ teaspoons (7 mL) freshly ground pepper
- 1 (15-ounce / 425 g) can artichoke hearts, quartered, or 1 bag frozen artichoke hearts
- ¼ cup (60 mL) water
- 1 small lemon, sliced as thinly as possible, about 10 slices
- 4 sprigs of fresh oregano, finely chopped

1. Preheat the oven to 350°F (180°C).
2. In a large sauté pan, heat 2 tablespoons (30 mL) of the olive oil over medium-high heat.
3. Sprinkle the halibut fillets with ½ teaspoon (2 mL) of the salt and 1 teaspoon (5 mL) of the pepper.
4. Place the fillets, flesh side (not skin side) down, in the pan.. Cook for about 5 minutes, and then remove the fillets and place them in a shallow baking dish. Set the sauté pan aside.
5. Put the fish in the oven and bake for about 12 minutes, until the fish is cooked through.
6. In the sauté pan used for the fillets, add the artichokes and water and cook, stirring, for 5 minutes.
7. Add the lemon slices, oregano, and the remaining 2 tablespoons (30 mL) of the olive oil, the remaining ½ teaspoon (2 mL) of the salt, and the remaining ½ teaspoon (2 mL) of the pepper and bake for another 5 minutes.
8. Remove the halibut from the oven and pour the lemon and artichoke mixture over top of each fillet.

Top: Spring-Green Tuna Pasta (page 48)

Blackened Whitefish

Yield: 2 servings

The spice mix in this recipe can also be used as a chicken rub or in a vegetable stir-fry.

- 1 tablespoon (15 mL) paprika
- 1 teaspoon (5 mL) chili powder
- ½ teaspoon (2 mL) dried oregano
- ½ teaspoon (2 mL) dried thyme
- ½ teaspoon (2 mL) sea salt
- ½ teaspoon (2 mL) freshly ground pepper
- ¼ teaspoon (1 mL) chili pepper flakes
- 3 tablespoons (45 mL) brown rice flour
- Juice of half a lemon
- 2 to 4 whitefish fillets, or tilapia, catfish, or sole, depending on the size and thickness
- 2 tablespoons (30 mL) sunflower oil

1. In a shallow dish, combine the paprika, chili powder, oregano, thyme, salt, pepper, chili pepper flakes, and flour.
2. Squeeze the lemon juice evenly over the fish fillets, and then dip them into the spice mixture. Coat both sides well.
3. In a large sauté pan, heat the sunflower oil over medium heat for a couple of minutes.
4. Add the fish fillets and cook, turning once, about 3 minutes per side, until the fish is opaque and easily flakes with a fork.

Spring-Green Tuna Pasta

Yield: 4 servings

The asparagus in this recipe adds a lovely green colour to the dish. Six spears of asparagus contain half the recommended daily intake of folic acid. Folic acid is a vitamin critical for pregnant mothers, since it protects against neural tube defects. It is also protective against heart disease, as it tames homocysteine.

- 6 to 8 cups (1.5 to 2 L) water
- 1 teaspoon (5 mL) sea salt
- 10 ounces (300 g) dry brown rice fusilli or penne (2 ounces / 60 g makes about 1 cup / 250 mL)
- 1 teaspoon (5 mL) plus ¼ cup (60 mL) extra-virgin olive oil
- ½ teaspoon (2 mL) chili pepper flakes
- 1 bunch of thin asparagus, cut into 2-inch (5 cm) pieces and the hard ends discarded
- 1 fennel bulb, cored, tops chopped off, and sliced
- ½ cup Parsley Pesto (page 88)
- 1 (6-ounce / 170 g) can chunk light tuna, drained

1. Put the water and salt in a large saucepan over high heat and bring to a boil. Add the pasta and the 1 teaspoon (5 mL) of olive oil and bring to a boil again.
2. Cook for 12 to 15 minutes, or until the pasta is chewy but not too soft.
3. While the pasta is cooking, heat the ¼ cup (60 mL) of olive oil and the chili flakes in a large sauté pan over medium heat for 2 minutes.
4. Add the asparagus and the fennel and cook, stirring occasionally, for another 5 minutes.
5. Add the parsley pesto, the tuna chunks, and a couple of tablespoons of the pasta cooking water. Cover, reduce the heat to low, and cook for another 5 minutes.
6. Once the pasta has finished cooking, drain the water and add the pasta to the sauté pan. Stir to combine well and heat through for 2 minutes before serving.

Tuna-Mango Rolls

Yield: 4 servings

Sunflower sprouts, an optional ingredient in this recipe, are hulled sunflower seeds that have been soaked and sprouted for a day or so. Sprouting activates the seeds, increasing enzyme levels and protein content and making them much easier to digest.

- 1 small avocado, diced
- Juice of 1 lime
- 2 teaspoons (10 mL) lime zest
- 1 (6-ounce / 170 g) can chunk light tuna, packed in water, or 1 cooked tuna steak, diced
- 1 small red bell pepper, seeded and diced
- 3 green onions, thinly sliced, white and pale green parts only
- 1 cup (250 mL) loosely packed, chopped fresh cilantro
- 1 teaspoon (5 mL) chili pepper flakes
- 8 (8½-inch / 21 cm) Vietnamese rice paper wrappers
- 2 cups (500 mL) sunflower sprouts, optional
- 1 large mango, thinly sliced (24 slices)

1. Combine the avocado, lime juice, lime zest, and tuna in small bowl. Stir in the red pepper, green onions, cilantro, and chili pepper flakes. Set aside.
2. Fill a large bowl with warm water. Submerge 1 rice paper wrapper in the water for 10 seconds, or just until it becomes soft. Remove the wrapper to a flat work surface, and let it rest for 30 seconds; it will become easier to handle.
3. Spoon ¼ cup (60 mL) of the avocado mixture onto the wrapper, just below the middle, leaving a 1-inch (2.5 cm) border on either side. Top with ¼ cup (60 mL) of the sprouts (if using) and 3 mango slices. Fold the bottom of the wrapper up over the filling, pressing the filling as you go. Fold both sides of the wrapper inward. Gently press to seal and roll the wrapper to the top edge. Repeat with the remaining wrappers.

Mains
Vegetarian

Adzuki Bean and Squash Sauté

Fresh Salad Rolls

Moroccan Stew

Quinoa and Chickpea Pilaf

Kale Rolls

Sesame Stir-Fry

Curried Lentil Stew

Chickpeas and Chard

Roasted Red Pepper and Avocado Roll

Adzuki Bean and Squash Sauté

Yield: 4 servings

If you are consuming soy on your detox, a gluten-free soy sauce, such as Bragg's, can be used in this recipe instead of the sea salt and lemon.

- 1 (15-ounce / 425 g) can adzuki beans, drained and rinsed, or ⅔ cup (160 mL) dried beans
- 3 tablespoons (45 mL) extra-virgin olive oil
- ½ yellow onion, diced
- 2 garlic cloves, minced
- 1 teaspoon (5 mL) chili pepper flakes
- 1 large butternut squash, diced into 1-inch cubes
- 1 cup (250 mL) water
- 1 small bunch of kale, chopped (about 2 cups / 500 mL)
- 1 tablespoon (15 mL) dried oregano
- 1 teaspoon (5 mL) sea salt
- 1 teaspoon (5 mL) freshly ground pepper
- Juice of half a lemon

1. If using dried adzuki beans, add 3 cups (750 mL) of water to a large saucepan with the adzuki beans, cover, and bring to a boil. Reduce the heat and simmer, covered, for another 60 minutes, or until the beans are tender.
2. Meanwhile, start on the rest of the dish by heating 1 tablespoon (15 mL) of the olive oil in a saucepan over medium-low heat. Add the onion, garlic, and chili flakes and cook, stirring constantly, being careful not to burn the garlic.
3. Add the squash and water, turn the heat up to medium, cover, and let cook for 20 minutes, or until the squash is tender (easily pierced with a fork).
4. Add the kale, oregano, salt, and pepper and cook for another 10 minutes before adding the cooked or canned adzuki beans.
5. Stir and let cook, covered, for another 15 minutes.
6. For the last minute of cooking, stir in the remaining 1 tablespoon (15 mL) of the olive oil and the lemon juice.

Fresh Salad Rolls

Yield: 4 servings

This recipe is fun to make with friends on a weekend when there is time to julienne the veggies. The Tangy Almond Dipping Sauce (page 89) is a delicious accompaniment to these salad rolls.

- 8 leaves of Boston Bibb lettuce
- 1 small red bell pepper, seeded and thinly sliced
- 1 small orange bell pepper, seeded and thinly sliced
- 2 carrots, peeled and julienned
- 3 green onions, thinly sliced, white and pale green parts only
- 1 cup (250 mL) loosely packed, chopped fresh cilantro
- 1 cup (250 mL) loosely packed, chopped fresh mint
- 1 cup (250 mL) finely chopped almonds
- ½ package thin rice vermicelli noodles or bean thread noodles, cooked
- 8 (8½-inch / 21 cm) Vietnamese rice paper wrappers

1. The easiest way to put together the salad rolls is to make an assembly line on the kitchen countertop or table, starting with the lettuce leaves.
2. Fill a large bowl with warm water. Submerge 1 rice paper wrapper in the water for 10 seconds, or just until it becomes soft. Remove the wrapper to a flat work surface, and let it rest for 30 seconds; it will become easier to handle.
3. Place 1 leaf of lettuce just below the middle of the wrapper, leaving a 1-inch (2.5 cm) border on each side. Top with ¼ cup (60 mL) of the noodles, then 2 or 3 slices each of the red pepper, orange pepper, and carrots. Sprinkle a few green onions and some cilantro and mint on the veggies, and then top with some of the almonds.
4. Fold the bottom of the wrapper up over the filling, pressing the filling as you go. Fold both sides of the wrapper inward. Gently press to seal and roll the wrapper to the top edge. Repeat with the remaining wrappers.

Moroccan Stew

Yield: 4 servings

A quick trip to a bulk store at the beginning of your detox can save you money and unnecessary waste. Not everyone has a full shelf of herbs and spices, or wants one, and this is one way to get just the amount you need! This stew is delicious served over brown rice or quinoa.

- 2 tablespoons (30 mL) sunflower oil
- 3 garlic cloves, minced
- 2 tablespoons (30 mL) peeled and minced fresh gingerroot
- ½ teaspoon (2 mL) chili pepper flakes
- ½ teaspoon (2 mL) cinnamon
- ½ teaspoon (2 mL) turmeric
- ½ teaspoon (2 mL) ground cumin
- ¼ teaspoon (1 mL) freshly ground pepper
- ¼ teaspoon (1 mL) allspice
- ¼ teaspoon (1 mL) ground coriander
- 1 large sweet potato, peeled and diced
- 2 small turnips, peeled and diced
- 1 medium zucchini, diced
- 2 carrots, peeled and diced
- ¼ small head of red or green cabbage, shredded
- ½ red bell pepper, seeded and diced
- 1 (19-ounce / 540 mL) can chickpeas, drained and rinsed
- 1 teaspoon (5 mL) sea salt
- ½ cup (125 mL) chopped fresh cilantro

1. Heat the oil in a large stockpot over medium heat. Add the garlic, ginger, chili pepper flakes, cinnamon, turmeric, cumin, pepper, allspice, and coriander. Stir for 5 minutes, or until lightly browned.
2. Add the sweet potato, turnips, zucchini, carrots, cabbage, and red pepper. Pour in enough water to just cover the vegetables, about 5 to 6 cups (1.25 to 1.5 L).
3. Cover and cook for 25 to 30 minutes, or until the vegetables are tender but not fully cooked.
4. Ladle out 1½ cups (375 mL) of the vegetables and 1½ cups (375 mL) of the broth and purée in a food processor or blender until thick. Add back to the stew.
5. Mix in the chickpeas and the salt and bring to a simmer. Cook, covered, for 10 to 15 minutes.
6. Stir in the cilantro and serve over brown rice or quinoa.

Quinoa and Chickpea Pilaf

Yield: 4 servings

Try to make the Basic Vegetable Stock (page 34) or a chicken stock before you start your detox and freeze for future use. This is more economical than buying stock, and it ensures that all the ingredients that go into making the stock are detox-friendly!

- 1½ cups (375 mL) quinoa
- 1 large sweet potato, unpeeled, washed, and diced
- 2 tablespoons (30 mL) extra-virgin olive oil
- ½ teaspoon (2 mL) sea salt
- 3 cups (750 mL) vegetable or chicken stock or water
- 2 garlic cloves, minced
- ½ teaspoon (2 mL) chili pepper flakes
- 1 (19-ounce / 540 mL) can chickpeas, drained and rinsed
- 1 cup (250 mL) green beans, steamed
- ¼ cup (60 mL) sunflower seeds
- ½ cup (125 mL) chopped fresh flat-leaf parsley, or 1 tablespoon (15 mL) dried parsley
- 1 teaspoon (5 mL) freshly ground pepper

1. Preheat the oven to 450°F (230°C).
2. Rinse the quinoa to get rid of the soapy outer covering, drain, and set aside.
3. Place the sweet potato on a baking sheet and drizzle with the olive oil and sprinkle with the salt and roast in the oven for 30 minutes.
4. Bring the stock to a boil in a large saucepan or stockpot, and add the quinoa, garlic, and chili pepper flakes. Cover and let simmer for about 15 minutes, until most of the water is absorbed and the quinoa is soft but a little "al dente."
5. Add the chickpeas, green beans, sweet potato, and sunflower seeds, and cook, stirring, until heated through, about 5 minutes.
6. Stir in the parsley and pepper just before serving.

Kale Rolls

Yield: 4 servings

These rolls are also delicious when filled with Quinoa and Chickpea Pilaf (page 56). Make sure to buy large kale leaves to allow for easy rolling. If using canned beans, cook the beans, sage, sea salt, and pepper together in a sauté pan over medium heat for 5 minutes, until heated through, before adding the garlic and olive oil.

- 1½ cups (375 mL) dried white beans such as navy or Great Northern
- 20 fresh sage leaves
- 1 teaspoon (5 mL) sea salt
- 1 teaspoon (5 mL) freshly ground pepper
- 2 garlic cloves, minced, plus 1 garlic clove, minced
- 3 tablespoons (45 mL) extra-virgin olive oil
- 8 large kale leaves, washed, stems removed and reserved
- ½ cup (125 mL) vegetable or chicken stock

1. Put the dried beans in a large saucepan and add water to cover by 2 inches and bring to a boil over high heat.
2. Add the sage leaves, reduce the heat to low, and cover. Cook until the beans begin to soften.
3. Add the salt and pepper and continue cooking until the beans are very tender.
4. If necessary, drain any remaining liquid, and then add the 2 minced garlic cloves and 1 tablespoon (15 mL) of the olive oil and cook for another 2 minutes. Set aside.
5. Coarsely chop the kale stems and place in a deep sauté pan with the remaining 2 tablespoons (30 mL) of olive oil and the 1 minced garlic clove. Cook over medium heat for 5 minutes, stirring occasionally. Remove the sauté pan from the heat.
6. Lay out a kale leaf, place 1 tablespoon (15 mL) of the bean mixture on the wide end of the leaf. Roll the leaf up and place it in the sauté pan on top of the garlic and stems.
7. Repeat Step 6 until all the kale leaves are used.
8. Pour the stock over the rolls and return the sauté pan to the stove over medium heat. When the stock begins to boil, turn the heat to low and cover. Cook for 10 minutes.
9. To serve, carefully spoon the rolls out and place them on serving plates. Top the rolls with the cooked kale stems, garlic, and pan juices.

Sesame Stir-Fry

Yield: 2 to 4 servings

Serve this stir-fry on top of quinoa or brown rice or to accompany a fish or chicken dish.

- 1 tablespoon (15 mL) sesame oil
- 1 tablespoon (15 mL) sunflower oil
- 2 garlic cloves, minced
- 2 tablespoons (30 mL) peeled and minced fresh gingerroot
- 1 teaspoon (5 mL) chili pepper flakes
- 1 red bell pepper, seeded and sliced
- 1 yellow bell pepper, seeded and sliced
- 1 green bell pepper, seeded and sliced
- 1 medium zucchini, sliced
- Juice of half a lime
- ½ teaspoon (2 mL) sea salt
- ½ teaspoon (2 mL) freshly ground pepper
- ¼ cup (60 mL) sesame seeds

1. Heat the sesame and sunflower oils in a large sauté pan over medium-low heat and add the garlic, ginger, and chili pepper flakes. Cook for 2 minutes, being careful not to burn the garlic.
2. Add the bell peppers and zucchini, stir, and cook, covered, for 10 minutes.
3. Stir in the lime juice, salt, pepper, and sesame seeds and cook for an additional 5 minutes.

Curried Lentil Stew

Yield: 4 servings

This stew is delicious served over brown rice or quinoa. Turmeric, one of the ingredients in this recipe, is one of nature's most powerful healers. The active ingredient in turmeric is curcumin. Long known for its anti-inflammatory properties, it also has anti-bacterial and anti-cancerous benefits.

- 3 tablespoons (45 mL) sunflower oil
- 1 small yellow onion, finely diced
- 1 teaspoon (5 mL) sea salt
- 2 tablespoons (30 mL) peeled and minced fresh gingerroot
- 3 garlic cloves, coarsely chopped
- 5 cups (1.25 L) water
- ¼ teaspoon (1 mL) chili pepper flakes
- 1 teaspoon (5 mL) curry powder
- ½ teaspoon (2 mL) turmeric
- ¼ teaspoon (1 mL) ground cumin
- 1 cup (250 mL) dried red lentils, rinsed and drained
- 3 large carrots, peeled and diced
- 2 cups (500 mL) loosely packed fresh spinach
- ¼ cup (60 mL) loosely packed, chopped fresh cilantro
- 1 teaspoon (5 mL) freshly ground pepper

1. Heat the sunflower oil in a large sauté pan over medium heat. Add the onion and ½ teaspoon (2 mL) of the salt, and cook, stirring occasionally, for 10 minutes.
2. Purée the ginger, garlic, and ¼ cup (60 mL) of the water in a small food processor, and then add the purée to the onion in the sauté pan. Cook for 5 minutes more.
3. Add the chili flakes, curry, turmeric, and cumin and cook, stirring, for 1 minute.
4. Stir in the lentils and the remaining 4¾ cups (965 mL) of the water, cover, and cook over low heat for 30 minutes.
5. Add the carrots and the remaining ½ teaspoon (2 mL) of salt and simmer for an additional 20 minutes.
6. Stir in the spinach and simmer, uncovered, for 5 minutes.
7. Stir in the cilantro and pepper. More water can be added to thin out the stew to easily pour over brown rice or quinoa.

Chickpeas and Chard

Yield: 4 servings

Swiss chard's flavour is associated with its oxalic acid content, similar to that is found in spinach and rhubarb. Chard and beet greens are interchangeable in most recipes. This dish can be served on its own or over brown rice.

- 8 ounces (250 g) dried chickpeas, soaked overnight
- 1 small yellow onion, unpeeled and cut in half
- 1 bay leaf
- 1 whole clove
- ½ teaspoon (2 mL) sea salt
- 1 teaspoon (5 mL) freshly ground pepper
- 1 bunch of Swiss chard, coarsely chopped
- 2 garlic cloves, minced
- 2 tablespoons (30 mL) extra-virgin olive oil
- ½ cup (125 mL) chopped toasted almonds

1. Drain and rinse the soaked chickpeas and put them in a large saucepan and cover with water by 2 inches. Place on the stove over high heat, uncovered, and bring to a boil.
2. Add the onion, bay leaf, and clove to the saucepan, reduce the heat to low, and simmer, partially covered, for 60 minutes.
3. Sprinkle with the salt and pepper and continue to cook, stirring occasionally, until the beans are tender but still intact. Add more water if necessary.
4. Add the chard and cook for another 20 minutes. Add more water if a thinner consistency is desired.
5. Remove the onion, bay leaf, and clove.
6. Add the garlic and olive oil and stir. Top with toasted almonds.
7. Serve as is or on top of brown rice.

Roasted Red Pepper and Avocado Roll

Yield: 4 servings

Roasting red peppers deepens the flavour and removes the skin. If you have never roasted red peppers, it's really easy! Cut the peppers in half and clean out the seeds. Place them on a baking sheet skin side up. Place the sheet in the oven under the broiler. The skin will start to blacken and soften in 7 to 10 minutes. Once the skins are brownish-black, remove the peppers from the oven and immediately place them in a large Ziploc bag. Close and let sit for 20 minutes, or until the peppers have time to cool and "sweat." Once they have cooled, you will be able to peel the skins right off.

- 4 nori seaweed sheets
- 2 cups (500 mL) cooked and cooled short-grain brown rice*
- 1 avocado, peeled and cut into thin strips
- 2 red bell peppers, roasted and cooled and cut into thin strips
- 1 English cucumber, peeled and seeded and cut into thin strips
- 8 tablespoons (125 mL) sesame seeds, toasted

*See Appendix 1, "How to Cook Whole Grains"

1. Place 1 sheet of nori, shiny side down, on a bamboo sushi mat.
2. Spread ½ cup (125 mL) of the rice in a thin layer over the sheet of nori, leaving about a 2-inch (5 cm) strip uncovered at the top edge (the edge furthest away from you) of the sheet. Make a slight depression with your fingers across the middle of the rice.
3. Neatly lay a strip of the red pepper, avocado, and cucumber in the groove in the rice that you made with your fingers, and sprinkle 1 tablespoon (15 mL) of the sesame seeds over top.
4. To roll, pick up the edges of the mat and the nori together and begin to roll slowly, using medium pressure to tuck in the filling, and taking care not to let the mat catch in the roll, to create a compact tube. The moisture from the filling will enable the nori to stick together.
5. Remove the mat from around the roll and place it on a cutting board. Leave the roll, seam side down, while you assemble the remaining 3 nori sheets.
6. Using a wet, sharp knife, slice each roll into 6 equal pieces.

Sides
Grains

Crunchy Brown Rice with Pears

Carrot Quinoa

Quinoa Pilaf

Kasha with Onions

Socca Bread

Quinoa Crispbread

Crunchy Brown Rice with Pears

Yield: 4 servings

Did you know that the milling process that converts brown rice to white rice removes 80% of the vitamin B1, 90% of the vitamin B6, and 60% of the iron?

- 3 tablespoons (45 mL) extra-virgin olive oil
- ½ cup (125 mL) finely chopped yellow onion
- 2 garlic cloves, minced
- 2 medium carrots, diced
- 1 cup (250 mL) brown basmati rice
- 2 cups (500 mL) chicken or vegetable stock
- 1 teaspoon (5 mL) chopped fresh thyme
- 2 celery stalks, diced
- 2 pears, peeled and diced
- ½ cup (125 mL) walnut pieces, toasted
- ½ teaspoon (2 mL) sea salt
- 1 teaspoon (5 mL) freshly ground pepper
- 2 green onions, finely sliced

1. In a medium saucepan, heat the olive oil over medium heat.
2. Add the onions and garlic and cook, stirring, until translucent, about 5 minutes.
3. Add the carrots and cook until tender, another 5 minutes.
4. Add the rice and stir to coat, and then add the stock and bring to a boil over high heat. Reduce the heat to low, cover, and let simmer until the rice is tender, about 30 minutes.
5. When the rice is tender, remove from the heat and stir in the thyme, celery, pears, and walnuts.
6. Cover and let stand another 5 minutes. Stir in the salt and pepper and garnish with the green onions.

Carrot Quinoa

Yield: 4 servings

Quinoa (pronounced "keen-wah") has been produced in the Andes Mountains in South America for thousands of years and is still sometimes referred to as "the gold of the Incas." Quinoa is one of two plant-based foods that contain all nine essential amino acids, making it a fabulous source of protein!

- 1 tablespoon (15 mL) extra-virgin olive oil
- 1 small yellow onion, finely diced
- 2 celery stalks, finely diced
- 1 zucchini, finely diced
- 2 carrots, finely diced
- 1 cup (250 mL) freshly juiced carrot juice or pure bottled carrot juice
- 1 cup (250 mL) water
- 1 cup (250 mL) quinoa
- ½ teaspoon (2 mL) dried thyme
- Pinch of nutmeg
- ½ teaspoon (2 mL) sea salt
- ½ teaspoon (2 mL) freshly ground pepper

1. Heat the olive oil in a large saucepan over medium heat for 1 minute.
2. Add the onion, celery, zucchini, and carrots. Cover and cook until the vegetables soften, about 5 minutes.
3. Stir in the carrot juice and water and bring to a boil, uncovered, over medium heat. Stir in the quinoa, thyme, nutmeg, salt, and pepper. Reduce the heat to low and simmer, covered, until the liquid has been absorbed and the quinoa is tender, about 20 minutes.

Quinoa Pilaf

Yield: 4 servings

Someone with diagnosed celiac disease is unable to eat gluten, as it damages the small intestine, reducing the absorption of nutrients. Gluten is the protein portion of wheat, rye, barley, and oats. Quinoa is a gluten-free grain.

- 2 tablespoons (30 mL) extra-virgin olive oil
- 1 small yellow onion, finely diced
- 3 garlic cloves, minced
- 1 large carrot, diced
- 1 red bell pepper, seeded and diced
- 2 cups (500 mL) quinoa
- 4 cups (1 L) water or vegetable stock
- 1 cup (250 mL) frozen peas, thawed
- ½ teaspoon (2 mL) sea salt
- 1 teaspoon (5 mL) freshly ground pepper

1. Heat the olive oil in a sauté pan over medium heat, and then add the onion. Cook, stirring, until tender and golden in colour, about 5 minutes.
2. Add the garlic, carrots, and bell pepper and cook for another 5 minutes.
3. Add the quinoa and water or stock and bring to a boil, uncovered, over high heat.
4. Reduce the heat to low and simmer, covered, for 20 minutes.
5. Stir in the peas and salt and pepper and let sit, covered, for 5 minutes before serving.

Socca Bread

Yield: 1 (20-inch / 50 cm) circular flatbread

Socca bread is a quick bread that is made from chickpea flour, so it's gluten-free! It is crispy and has a mild smoky flavour and must be enjoyed fresh and hot, hot, hot, never reheated. It resembles cardboard in appearance, but don't be fooled, it's delicious, especially with Basic Hummus (page 86).

* 1 cup (250 mL) chickpea flour
* 1 teaspoon (5 mL) sea salt
* 2 teaspoons (10 mL) freshly ground pepper
* 1 cup (250 mL) room-temperature water
* 5 tablespoons (75 mL) extra-virgin olive oil
* ¼ cup (60 mL) chopped rosemary
* ½ small yellow onion, finely diced

1. Sift the chickpea flour into a medium mixing bowl and stir in the salt and pepper.
2. Gradually pour in the water, stirring constantly to remove any lumps.
3. Slowly stir in 2 tablespoons (30 mL) of the olive oil and mix until a runny dough forms.
4. Mix in the rosemary and onion, cover the bowl, and set aside overnight.
5. Preheat the oven to 450°F (230°C). When the oven is heated, place a 20-inch (50 cm) pizza pan or a baking sheet in the oven to heat for 5 minutes.
6. Remove the pan from the oven and pour 2 tablespoons (30 mL) of the olive oil evenly over the pizza pan, and then pour the dough into the pan (it should be about ¼ inch / 0.5 cm thick) and bake for 10 minutes.
7. Remove the pan from the oven and turn on the broiler to high-broil.
8. Lightly brush the bread with the remaining 1 tablespoon (15 mL) of the olive oil and place it under the broiler for 1 minute, or until golden brown.
9. Slice the bread into wedges and serve hot.

Kasha with Onions

Yield: 4 servings

Kasha, or roasted buckwheat groats, is not related to wheat, despite its name, and is naturally gluten-free. Buckwheat groats are the hulled, crushed kernels of buckwheat seeds.

* 2 medium yellow onions, chopped
* 6 tablespoons (90 mL) sunflower oil
* 1 cup (250 mL) kasha
* 1 teaspoon (5 mL) sea salt
* 1 teaspoon (5 mL) freshly ground pepper
* 2 cups (500 mL) vegetable stock or water, warmed
* 1 teaspoon (5 mL) dried thyme
* 1 tablespoon (15 mL) fresh flat-leaf parsley

1. In a medium sauté pan, cook the onion, without oil, over medium heat for 15 minutes.
2. Add 3 tablespoons (45 mL) of the sunflower oil, increase the heat to medium-high, and cook, stirring, for another 15 minutes. Set aside.
3. In a large sauté pan, heat the remaining 3 tablespoons (45 mL) of sunflower oil over medium-high heat. When the oil is hot, add the kasha, salt, and pepper and cook, stirring, for about 2 minutes.
4. Reduce the heat to low and slowly stir in the stock or water. Cover and cook for about 15 minutes.
5. Turn off the heat and stir in the onions, thyme, and parsley.

Quinoa Crispbread

Yield: 24 to 36 pieces

To make the rolling of the dough for this recipe easier, try placing a piece of parchment paper on top of the dough before rolling it with the rolling pin. The thickness of the dough should be less than ¼ inch (0.5 cm). To keep the crispbread fresh for two weeks, store in a stainless steel tin.

- 2 cups (500 mL) quinoa flour
- 2 cups (500 mL) flaked or rolled quinoa
- 1 cup (250 mL) roasted sesame seeds
- ½ cup (125 mL), heaping, sunflower or pumpkin seeds
- ½ cup (125 mL), heaping, grated almonds or hazelnuts
- ¼ cup (60 mL) flaxseeds
- 2 teaspoons (10 mL) sea salt
- 6 tablespoons (90 mL) sunflower oil
- 1 ½ cups (375 mL) cold water

1. Preheat the oven to 475°F (240°C).
2. Combine the quinoa flour, flaked quinoa, sesame seeds, sunflower seeds, almonds, flaxseeds, and salt in a large mixing bowl.
3. Add the oil and water and mix to make a thick dough. Divide the dough in half.
4. Dust a rolling pin with flour and roll out each half of the dough onto separate baking sheets lined with parchment paper.
5. Cut the dough into 4-inch (10 cm) squares, without cutting all the way through.
6. Place the baking sheets in the oven and bake for 7 minutes.
7. Reduce the heat to 350°F (180°C) while the dough is still in the oven and bake for another 20 to 25 minutes, until the crispbread is lightly browned around the edges.
8. Remove the crispbread immediately from the baking sheet and cool completely on a wire rack before storing.

Top: Crunchy Broccoli (page 75)
Bottom Left: Sweet Potato Fries (page 77)
Bottom Right: Pecan Brussels Sprouts (page 72)

Sides
Veggies

Vegetable Fritters

Pecan Brussels Sprouts

Asian Asparagus

Beet Greens

Sugar Snap Peas with Ginger and Garlic

Crunchy Broccoli

Oven-Roasted Squash

Roasted Root Vegetables

Sweet Potato Fries

Roasted Beets

Kale Done Simply

Green Beans and Almonds

Braised Cauliflower

Vegetable Fritters

Yield: 4 servings

This is a detox version of the traditional potato latke. Just don't eat this version with sour cream!

- 1 small red onion, peeled
- 1 large sweet potato, peeled
- 1 zucchini, trimmed
- 1 tablespoon (15 mL) finely chopped fresh parsley
- 1 cup (250 mL) chickpea flour
- 1 flax egg replacer*
- ½ tsp (2 mL) chili pepper flakes
- 1 teaspoon (5 mL) sea salt
- 1 teaspoon (5 mL) freshly ground pepper
- Sunflower oil for frying

*To make the flax egg replacer, combine 1 tablespoon (15 mL) of ground flaxseed with 3 tablespoons (45 mL) of water and let it sit for 2 minutes.

1. Preheat the oven to 300°F (150°C).
2. Using a hand grater or a food processor, shred the onion, sweet potato, and zucchini and place in a colander. Press out the liquid and transfer the vegetables to a large bowl.
3. Stir in the parsley, flour, egg replacer, chili pepper flakes, salt, and pepper, and mix well.
4. Pour a thin layer of oil in a large sauté pan and heat over medium-high heat. Scoop out a large spoonful of the vegetable mixture and tightly pack it with your hands. Place the fritter in the hot pan, gently flatten it with the back of a fork, and cook it for about 5 minutes on each side, until golden brown on both sides. Repeat with the rest of the vegetable mixture.
5. Drain the cooked fritters on paper towels and place them on a baking sheet. Transfer to the oven and bake for 10 minutes to finish cooking.

Pecan Brussels Sprouts

Yield: 4 servings

Brussels sprouts are a great source of vitamin C and have cancer-fighting compounds called indoles, as do other cruciferous vegetables.

- 4 cups (1 L) Brussels sprouts
- 1 large shallot
- 2 cups (500 mL) water
- ¼ cup (60 mL) sunflower oil
- 2 teaspoons (10 mL) dried parsley
- ½ cup (125 mL) chopped pecans
- 1 teaspoon (5 mL) sea salt
- 1 teaspoon (5 mL) freshly ground pepper

1. Cut the hard ends off the Brussels sprouts.
2. In a food processor, shred the Brussels sprouts and shallots.
3. Put the Brussels sprouts, shallots, and water in a large sauté pan, cover, and cook over high heat for 5 minutes, or until the Brussels sprouts are tender and the water is gone.
4. Stir in the sunflower oil, parsley, pecans, salt, and pepper. Cover and simmer over low heat for 10 minutes.

Beet Greens

Yield: 4 servings

Next time you buy beets, don't throw away the top leafy green portion. These leafy greens are just as nutritious as the beetroot!

- 2 bunches of beet greens
- 2 tablespoons (30 mL) extra-virgin olive oil
- 1 large shallot, finely diced
- ¼ cup (60 mL) water
- ¼ teaspoon (1 mL) sea salt
- 1 teaspoon (5 mL) freshly ground pepper

1. Wash the beet greens and stems well and chop coarsely.
2. Heat a sauté pan over medium-low heat. Add the olive oil and shallots, cover, and cook for 2 minutes, until the shallots are tender.
3. Add the beet greens and the water, salt, and pepper. Cover and cook for 5 minutes, or until the greens are wilted.

Asian Asparagus

Yield: 2 to 4 servings

Sunflower oil is light in taste and appearance and contains more vitamin E than any other vegetable oil. It has a combination of healthful monounsaturated and polyunsaturated fats.

- 1 bunch of asparagus
- ½ cup (125 mL) water
- 1 teaspoon (5 mL) sesame oil
- 1 teaspoon (5 mL) sunflower oil
- 1 teaspoon (5 mL) freshly ground pepper
- ½ teaspoon (2 mL) sea salt
- 2 tablespoons (30 mL) sesame seeds

1. Wash the asparagus and break off the hard ends.
2. Put the asparagus and water in a large sauté pan and place on the stove over medium-high heat. Cover and steam for 3 minutes.
3. Uncover, reduce the heat to low, and add the sesame and sunflower oils, salt, pepper, and sesame seeds. Stir to coat and cook, uncovered, for another 5 minutes.

Sugar Snap Peas with Ginger and Garlic

Yield: 2 servings

Sugar snap peas have "strings," similar to celery. Before eating raw or stir-frying, make sure to snap the stems to remove the stringy spines on both sides.

- 1 tablespoon (15 mL) extra-virgin olive oil
- 2 small shallots, finely diced
- 1 tablespoon (15 mL) peeled and minced fresh gingerroot
- 1 garlic clove, minced
- 2 cups (500 mL) sugar snap peas
- ¼ cup (60 mL) water
- ½ teaspoon (2 mL) sea salt
- ½ teaspoon (2 mL) freshly ground pepper
- 1 tablespoon (15 mL) chopped fresh mint

1. Heat the olive oil in a large sauté pan or wok over medium heat.
2. Add the shallots, gingerroot, and garlic and stir constantly for 1 minute.
3. Add the peas and cook, stirring, for 2 minutes.
4. Add the water, cover, and simmer until the peas are crisp yet tender, about 2 minutes.
5. Uncover, sprinkle the salt, pepper, and mint over top, stir through, and cook for another 2 minutes before serving.

Crunchy Broccoli

Yield: 2 servings

Mom was always right in making you eat your broccoli! It truly is a super food, filled with vitamins C and A and folic acid. A serving of broccoli contains almost as much calcium as a glass of milk! You can save the broccoli stalks trimmed from the florets in this recipe and use them in a soup or stock.

- 1 head of broccoli
- 2 tablespoons (30 mL) ground flaxseed
- 2 tablespoons (30 mL) sesame seeds
- 3 tablespoons (45 mL) extra-virgin olive oil
- ½ teaspoon (2 mL) sea salt
- ½ teaspoon (2 mL) freshly ground pepper

1. Preheat the oven to 500°F (260°C).
2. Cut the broccoli into bite-sized florets and soak in a bowl of water for 5 minutes.
3. Drain the water from the bowl and add the flaxseed, sesame seeds, olive oil, salt, and pepper and mix thoroughly.
4. Place the mixture on a baking sheet and bake in the oven for 15 minutes.

Roasted Root Vegetables

Yield: 4 servings

This recipe can also be turned into a root vegetable mash by adding warmed chicken broth or rice milk to the cooked vegetables and whipping them with a hand mixer.

- 3 large carrots, diced into 1-inch (2.5 cm) pieces
- 3 large parsnips, diced into 1-inch (2.5 cm) pieces
- 1 sweet potato, diced into 1-inch (2.5 cm) pieces
- 1 butternut squash, diced into 1-inch (2.5 cm) pieces
- 3 tablespoons (45 mL) extra-virgin olive oil
- 1 teaspoon (5 mL) sea salt
- ½ teaspoon (2 mL) freshly ground pepper
- 2 tablespoons (30 mL) chopped fresh parsley, or 2 teaspoons (10 mL) dried parsley

1. Preheat the oven to 425°F (220°C).
2. Place the carrots, parsnips, sweet potato, and squash in a large mixing bowl.
3. Sprinkle the olive oil over the vegetables, season with the salt and pepper, and mix thoroughly.
4. Place the vegetables on a baking sheet and bake for 35 minutes, or until the vegetables are tender when pierced with a fork.
5. Remove from the oven and sprinkle with the parsley just before serving.

Oven-Roasted Squash

Yield: 4 servings

Beta-carotene is a potent antioxidant that is found in squash that can help prevent the oxidation of cholesterol in the body. Since oxidized cholesterol can build up in blood vessels, contributing to the risk of heart disease and stroke, extra beta-carotene in the diet can help reduce the progression of atherosclerosis.

- 1 acorn squash or butternut squash
- ½ teaspoon (2 mL) sea salt
- 1 teaspoon (5 mL) freshly ground pepper
- 2 teaspoons (10 mL) dried oregano
- 2 tablespoons (30 mL) extra-virgin olive oil

1. Preheat the oven to 450°F (230°C).
2. Cut the squash in half and scoop out the seeds.
3. Cut the squash halves again so there are 4 pieces and place them on a baking sheet.
4. Sprinkle the squash evenly with the salt, pepper, and oregano.
5. Drizzle the olive oil over the squash and place in the oven. Bake for 45 minutes, or until the squash is tender when pierced with a fork.

Sweet Potato Fries

Yield: 2 servings

Why buy frozen white potato French fries when you can have nutritious and flavourful sweet potato fries in less than 20 minutes?

- 1 large sweet potato, cut into pieces 2 inches (5 cm) long and ½ inch (1 cm) wide.
- 3 tablespoons (45 mL) extra-virgin olive oil
- 1 garlic clove, minced
- ½ teaspoon (2 mL) paprika
- ½ teaspoon (2 mL) dried rosemary
- ½ teaspoon (2 mL) sea salt
- ½ teaspoon (2 mL) freshly ground pepper

1. Preheat the oven to 450°F (230°C).
2. Place the sweet potatoes in a large mixing bowl and add the olive oil, garlic, paprika, rosemary, salt, and pepper. Toss to evenly coat.
3. Place the potatoes on a baking sheet and bake in the oven for 20 minutes, or until the potatoes are easily pierced with a fork.
4. Remove from the oven, heat the broiler to high-broil, and place the potatoes under the broiler to finish with a quick 1-minute blast.

Roasted Beets

Yield: 4 servings

The reddish-purple hue of beets is thanks to a cancer-fighting pigment called betacyanin. Beets' effectiveness against colon cancer has been demonstrated in several studies. Don't forget to keep the leafy greens that are usually attached to the beetroots and steam or stir-fry them like you would with Swiss chard. When not on the Delicious Detox, you can add 1 tablespoon (15 mL) of honey and 1 tablespoon (15 mL) of balsamic vinegar to the beets and shallots, which caramelizes them, making them extra special!

- 1 tablespoon (15 mL) plus 1 teaspoon (5 mL) sea salt
- 8 medium-sized beets, scrubbed clean, both ends trimmed
- 3 tablespoons (45 mL) extra-virgin olive oil
- 1 teaspoon (5 mL) freshly ground pepper
- 1 large shallot, thinly sliced
- Juice of 1 lemon

1. Bring a large stockpot of water and the 1 tablespoon (15 mL) of salt to a boil over high heat.
2. Add the beets, cover the pot, and reduce the heat to medium-low. Simmer the beets until they are easily pierced with a fork, about 45 minutes.
3. Drain the beets and cover with ice-cold water.
4. Preheat the oven to 475°F (240°C).
5. Drain the beets again and peel them (the peels should be easy to remove). Place the peeled beets on a baking sheet.
6. In a small bowl, combine the olive oil, pepper, shallots, lemon juice, and the 1 teaspoon (5 mL) of salt, and pour over the beets to coat.
7. Place the beets in the oven and roast for 10 minutes.

Green Beans and Almonds

Yield: 2 servings

The vitamin K provided in green beans is quite important for strong bones. Vitamin K prevents excessive activation of osteoclasts—the cells responsible for breaking down bone.

* 3 cups (750 mL) green string beans, both ends trimmed
* ¼ cup (60 mL) water
* 2 tablespoons (30 mL) extra-virgin olive oil
* 1 garlic clove, minced
* ¼ cup (60 mL) toasted slivered almonds

1. Put the water and beans in a sauté pan over medium heat and cover. Cook for 5 minutes.
2. Uncover and add the olive oil, garlic, and almonds and cook, stirring, for 3 minutes.

Kale Done Simply

Yield: 2 to 4 servings

Kale is packed with calcium, fibre, iron, vitamin K, and vitamin C, definitely rating it among the best in super foods. Here it is briefly sautéed, but you can also include it raw, as in the Chickpea Slaw (page 22), or puréed and used in soups, as in the Puréed Mung Bean Soup (page 32).

* 1 bunch of kale, washed, coarsely chopped, and coarse stems removed
* ¼ cup (60 mL) extra-virgin olive oil
* 2 garlic cloves, minced
* ½ small yellow onion, thinly sliced
* 1 teaspoon (5 mL) chili pepper flakes
* ½ teaspoon (2 mL) sea salt
* 1 teaspoon (5 mL) freshly ground pepper

1. Pour a couple of inches of water into a large saucepan and place a steamer basket or colander on top and fill with the kale. Cover and put on the stove over high heat.
2. Steam for about 5 minutes, or until the kale is bright green and tender.
3. Heat the olive oil in a sauté pan over medium heat. Add the garlic, onions, and chili pepper flakes and cook for 5 minutes.
4. Add the kale and salt and pepper to the sauté pan and stir through for another minute.

Braised Cauliflower

Yield: 2 servings

Braising is a cooking technique in which the main ingredient is seared over high heat, and then simmered in liquid over low heat. Usually done with less expensive cuts of meat, it produces a more tender and flavourful meat. Braised cauliflower is delicious when paired with the Lemon and Artichoke Halibut (page 47).

- ¼ cup (60 mL) extra-virgin olive oil
- 2 garlic cloves, minced
- 1 medium head of cauliflower, trimmed and broken into small florets
- ¼ cup (60 mL) water
- Zest and juice of 1 lemon
- ¼ cup (60 mL) loosely packed, chopped fresh parsley, plus more for garnish
- ½ teaspoon (2 mL) sea salt
- ½ teaspoon (2 mL) freshly ground pepper

1. Heat the olive oil in a large sauté pan over medium heat. Add the garlic and cook for 1 minute.
2. Add the cauliflower and water, cover the pan, and cook for 15 minutes, or until the cauliflower is tender. Stir occasionally.
3. Uncover, increase the heat to high, and stir in the lemon zest and juice, salt, and pepper. Cook for 1 minute.
4. Garnish with parsley and serve.

Basic Hummus (page 86)

Dressings, Dips, and Snacks

Tahini-Lemon Dressing

Yield: ⅓ cup (80 mL)

Tahini is a paste made from crushed sesame seeds, and it has a very nutty taste. Tahini is a great source of calcium and essential fatty acids. This dressing is delicious on steamed kale with a sprinkling of sesame seeds.

- 1 garlic clove, coarsely chopped
- ½ teaspoon (2 mL) sea salt
- ½ teaspoon (2 mL) freshly ground pepper
- Juice of half a lemon
- 1 tablespoon (15 mL) tahini
- 3 tablespoons (45 mL) extra-virgin olive oil
- 1 teaspoon (5 mL) water

1. In a food processor, blender, or mini chopper, mince the garlic with the salt and pepper.
2. Add the lemon juice and tahini and pulse.
3. Slowly add the olive oil and water and blend well.

Avocado Dressing

Yield: ½ cup (125 mL)

In addition to making a delicious dressing, avocado can be used to make a nutritive face mask. The next time you have some extra avocado, just add 1 tablespoon (15 mL) of honey and 1 tablespoon (15 mL) of plain yogurt to whatever avocado you have leftover and mash together. Apply the mask for 15 minutes, remove with warm water, and dry. Fantastic for dry or mature skin!

- 1 small garlic clove, coarsely chopped
- ½ teaspoon (2 mL) sea salt
- ½ teaspoon (2 mL) freshly ground pepper
- ¼ teaspoon (1 mL) cayenne
- 1 ripe avocado, peeled and pitted
- Juice of half a lemon
- ¼ cup (60 mL) water

1. In a food processor or blender, mince the garlic with the salt, pepper, and cayenne.
2. Add the avocado and pulse until well blended.
3. Slowly add the lemon juice and water and pulse until smooth.

Ginger-Lime Dressing

Yield: 1 cup (250 mL)

Instead of using bottled stir-fry sauces, try using this dressing next time you want to quickly sauté some peppers.

* 1 green onion, coarsely chopped
* 1 (1-inch / 2.5 cm) piece of fresh gingerroot, peeled
* 1 garlic clove, coarsely chopped
* Juice of 1 lime
* 2 tablespoons (30 mL) sesame oil
* ½ teaspoon (2 mL) chili pepper flakes

1. In a food processor or blender, combine all the ingredients and pulse until blended well.

Artichoke and Sunflower Dip

Yield: 1½ cups (375 mL)

Adding roasted red peppers to the artichoke hearts while puréeing is another way to make this dip extra special.

* ½ cup (125 mL) raw, hulled sunflower seeds
* 1 (15-ounce / 425 g) can artichoke hearts, juice drained and reserved
* 2 garlic cloves, coarsely chopped
* 2 tablespoons (30 mL) extra-virgin olive oil
* 1 tablespoon (15 mL) minced fresh oregano, or teaspoon (5 mL) dried oregano
* 1 teaspoon (5 mL) chili pepper flakes
* ½ teaspoon (2 mL) sea salt
* ½ teaspoon (2 mL) freshly ground pepper

1. Place the sunflower seeds in a small bowl and cover with warm water. Let soak for several hours or overnight.
2. Drain the sunflower seeds, then purée them in a food processor or blender until smooth. Add the artichoke hearts and garlic and process until smooth.
3. Add the olive oil, oregano, chili pepper flakes, salt, and pepper and process until smooth. The reserved artichoke juice may be added if needed to thin out the dip.
4. Serve at once or transfer to a tightly covered bowl and refrigerate until ready to serve.

Guacamole

Yield: 1 cup (250 mL)

Guacamole is a great dip to use on Quinoa Crispbread (page 69) or with Kale Chips (page 90). If you don't mind a little heat, include the seeds of the jalapeño pepper in this recipe.

- 2 small ripe avocados, peeled and diced
- Juice of 1 lime
- 1 garlic clove, minced
- ½ small jalapeño pepper, seeded and minced
- 2 tablespoons (30 mL) finely chopped fresh cilantro
- ½ teaspoon (2 mL) sea salt
- 1 teaspoon (5 mL) freshly ground pepper

1. Mash the avocados with a fork in a medium bowl.
2. Add the jalapeño pepper, cilantro, salt, and pepper and continue mashing with a fork until well combined.

Basic Hummus

Yield: 2 cups (500 mL)

Before starting your detox plan, make sure you set aside a day to prep as many things possible to make your first week easy. Hummus is great to have on hand to snack on with veggies or rice crackers.

- 1 (19-ounce / 540 mL) can chickpeas, drained (reserve the liquid) and rinsed
- 2 garlic cloves, coarsely chopped
- 1 tablespoon (15 mL) tahini (sesame seed butter)
- Juice of 1 small lemon
- 1 teaspoon (5 mL) dried parsley
- 1 teaspoon (5 mL) paprika
- ½ teaspoon (2 mL) sea salt
- 1 teaspoon (5 mL) freshly ground pepper
- ¼ cup (60 mL) extra-virgin olive oil

1. In a food processor, combine the chickpeas, garlic, tahini, lemon juice, parsley, paprika, salt, and pepper. Pulse until combined.
2. With the processor running, slowly add the olive oil through the feed tube, continually pulsing until the mixture is smooth. If after a couple of minutes the hummus is still chunky, add some of the reserved chickpea liquid and process until the hummus is smooth.

Chermoula

Yield: 1 cup (250 mL)

Chermoula is a marinade typically used in Tunisian or Moroccan cooking to flavour fish. This recipe is delicious on a white fish such as halibut or cod that has been grilled with a sprinkle of sea salt and pepper.

- 2 cups (500 mL) chopped fresh cilantro
- 1 cup (250 mL) chopped fresh parsley
- 3 garlic cloves, coarsely chopped
- ½ teaspoon (2 mL) sea salt
- 2 teaspoons (10 mL) cumin seeds, toasted
- ½ teaspoon (2 mL) coriander seeds, toasted
- 1 teaspoon (5 mL) paprika
- ½ teaspoon (2 mL) cayenne
- ¼ to ½ cup (60 to 125 mL) extra-virgin olive oil
- Juice of 1 large lemon

1. In a food processor or blender, purée the cilantro and parsley. Remove and set aside.
2. In the same food processor or blender, purée the garlic and salt. Slowly add spoonfuls of the cilantro and parsley mixture and pulse until everything is well blended.
3. Add the cumin seeds, coriander seeds, paprika, cayenne, olive oil, and lemon juice and purée until smooth.

Mint Pesto

Yield: 1 cup (250 mL)

Mint is an excellent remedy for reducing symptoms related to digestion—indigestion, stomach cramps, gas, and nausea. They don't serve after-dinner mints at restaurants for nothing!

- 2 garlic cloves, coarsely chopped
- ½ cup (125 mL) almonds, toasted
- ½ teaspoon (2 mL) sea salt
- 2 cups (500 mL) loosely packed fresh mint
- ¼ cup (60 mL) extra-virgin olive oil

1. Put the garlic, almonds, and salt in a food processor.
2. Add the mint and process until finely minced.
3. With the machine running, slowly add the olive oil in a steady stream through the feed tube and process until the pesto is blended into a paste.
4. Transfer to a bowl, cover tightly, and refrigerate until ready to use.

Peach and Blueberry Salsa

Yield: 2 cups (500 mL)

Usually substituting fresh herbs for dried herbs makes a small difference in the taste of the recipe. This is one recipe where using fresh herbs is absolutely necessary.

- 1 mango, peeled and diced
- 2 medium peaches, peeled and diced
- ⅓ cup (80 mL) blueberries, halved
- 2 green onions, minced
- ¼ cup (60 mL) lime juice
- 1 garlic clove, minced
- 6 teaspoons (90 mL) minced fresh basil
- 1 tablespoon (15 mL) minced fresh sage
- 1 tablespoon (15 mL) extra-virgin olive oil

1. Gently combine the mango, peaches, blueberries, and green onions in a medium bowl.
2. In a separate bowl, whisk together the lime juice, garlic, basil, and sage. Add the olive oil, while whisking, and then pour over the peach mixture.
3. Toss to combine. Allow the flavours to blend at room temperature for about 1 hour before serving. This salsa can also be refrigerated overnight.

Parsley Pesto

Yield: 1 cup (250 mL)

Parsley is a powerful natural diuretic and is rich in vitamins A and C. It actually has more beta-carotene than a large carrot!

- 2 garlic cloves, coarsely chopped
- ½ cup (125 mL) walnuts, toasted
- ½ teaspoon (2 mL) sea salt
- 2 cups (500 mL) loosely packed, coarsely chopped fresh parsley
- ¼ cup (60 mL) extra-virgin olive oil

1. Put the garlic, walnuts, and salt in a food processor.
2. Add the parsley and process until finely minced.
3. With the machine running, slowly add the olive oil in steady stream through the feed tube and process until the pesto is blended into a paste.
4. Transfer to a bowl, cover tightly, and refrigerate until ready to use.

Tangy Almond Dipping Sauce

Yield: 1 cup (250 mL)

This dipping sauce is perfect to use with the Fresh Salad Rolls (page 54) or on top of steamed kale. Experiment using more or less almond butter and more or less water until the consistency of your liking is reached.

- 1 (2-inch / 5 cm) piece of fresh gingerroot, peeled and coarsely chopped
- 1 garlic clove, coarsely chopped
- 2 tablespoons (30 mL) almond butter
- Juice of 1 lime
- 1 teaspoon (5 mL) chili pepper flakes
- 1½ tablespoons (22.5 mL) sesame oil
- ½ cup (125 mL) water, or more if a more watery consistency is desired
- ¼ teaspoon (1 mL) sea salt

1. In a food processor or blender, mince the gingerroot and garlic.
2. Add the almond butter, lime juice, and chili pepper flakes and blend.
3. Lastly, add the sesame oil, water, and salt and blend until smooth.

Yellow-Pepper Sauce

Yield: 2 cups (500 mL)

Top a bowl of brown rice, lentils, and diced avocado with this easy-to-make sauce.

- 2 tablespoons (30 mL) extra-virgin olive oil
- 1 small yellow onion, chopped
- 3 yellow bell peppers, seeded and chopped
- ¼ to ½ cup (60 to 125 mL) water
- ½ teaspoon (2 mL) sea salt
- ½ teaspoon (2 mL) freshly ground pepper

1. Heat the olive oil in a saucepan over medium heat, and then add the onion. Cook, stirring, for a couple of minutes.
2. Add the bell pepper, cover, and cook for 5 minutes.
3. Add the water and season with the salt and pepper and cook, covered, for another 15 minutes.
4. Transfer the mixture to a food processor or blender and process until smooth.
5. Strain the blended mixture through a fine strainer back into the saucepan and heat through over medium heat for 1 minute. Serve immediately or transfer to an airtight container, cool to room temperature, and then refrigerate until ready to use.

Kale Chips

Yield: 2 to 4 servings

These are a great substitute for potato chips, and always a conversation starter at a party!

- 1 bunch of kale
- 1 tablespoon (15 mL) extra-virgin olive oil
- 1 teaspoon (5 mL) sea salt

1. Preheat the oven to 375°F (190°C).
2. Remove the stems from the kale.
3. Wash and dry the leaves and tear into bite-sized pieces.
4. Drizzle the leaves with the olive oil and sprinkle with the salt. Toss to thoroughly coat the leaves.
5. Line a baking sheet with parchment paper and place the kale leaves on top.
6. Bake in the oven for 10 to 15 minutes, until the edges are brown, but not burnt.

Roasted Apples

Yield: 2 cups (500 mL)

Roasted apples can be added to the Sweet Quinoa Porridge (page 17), used to top the Blueberry Buckwheat Pancakes (page 19), or just eaten as a snack!

- 3 apples (Granny Smith apples roast nicely, but any apple will do), peeled and diced
- 1 teaspoon (5 mL) cinnamon
- Juice of half a lemon

1. Preheat the oven to 400°F (200°C).
2. In a small bowl, combine the apples, cinnamon, and lemon juice and spread the mixture on a baking sheet.
3. Bake the apples for 20 minutes, remove from the oven, and let stand for 10 minutes if eating right away.
4. If storing, let stand until completely cooled and store in an airtight container for up to a week.

Chili Chickpeas

Yield: 3 to 4 servings

A tasty little afternoon snack if you want to spice up your day!

- 1 (19-ounce / 540 mL) can chickpeas, rinsed and drained
- 2 tablespoons (30 mL) extra-virgin olive oil
- ¾ teaspoon (4 mL) chili powder
- ¼ teaspoon (1 mL) ground cumin
- ¼ teaspoon (1 mL) sea salt
- ½ teaspoon (2 mL) freshly ground pepper

1. Preheat the oven to 300°F (150°C).
2. In a mixing bowl, combine the chickpeas with the olive oil, chili powder, cumin, salt, and pepper and toss to mix well.
3. Place the chickpea mixture on a baking sheet and bake for 30 to 40 minutes, stirring every 10 minutes, until crispy and dry.

How to Cook Whole Grains

- Rinse and drain the grain before cooking.
- Instead of cooking the grain with water, try using vegetable or chicken stock.
- Combine the grain and water in a saucepan and bring to a boil, uncovered. Cover and simmer over low heat for the required time listed below.

Cooking Time for Grains		
Grains	Water	Time (mins)
1 cup (250 mL) Amaranth	2 cups (500 mL)	20
1 cup (250 mL) Buckwheat	2 cups (500 mL)	20–30
1 cup (250 mL) Millet	2½ cups (625 mL)	30
1 cup (250 mL) Quinoa	2 cups (500 mL)	20
1 cup (250 mL) Brown Rice (long or short grain)	2 cups (500 mL)	25–35
1 cup (250 mL) Brown Basmati	2 cups (500 mL)	25–35
1 cup (250 mL) Wild Rice	2 cups (500 mL)	50–60

Appendix 2

How to Cook Dried Beans

- Rinse and drain the beans well before cooking. Pick out any pebbles.
- 1 cup (250 mL) of dried beans yields about 2½ cups (625 mL) of cooked beans.
- Dried beans cook faster if soaked overnight. Cover the beans with cold water by several inches in a large saucepan with a tight-fitting lid. Drain the beans after soaking and return to the saucepan with the required amount of water. Bring to a boil, cover, and let simmer on low heat for the cooking time listed below.
- Salt breaks down the skins of the beans, making them tough. Don't salt during soaking or early during the cooking time.

Cooking Time For Beans

Grains	Water	Soaked	Unsoaked
1 cup (250 mL) Adzuki Beans	2½ cups (625 mL)	60 minutes	120 minutes
1 cup (250 mL) Black Beans	3 cups (750 mL)	60 minutes	120 minutes
1 cup (250 mL) Chickpeas	4 cups (1 L)	120 minutes	180 minutes
1 cup (250 mL) Green/French Lentils	3 cups (750 mL)	0 minutes	40 minutes
1 cup (250 mL) Red Lentils	3 cups (750 mL)	20 minutes	20 minutes
1 cup (250 mL) Mung Beans	3½ cups (875 mL)	60 minutes	90 minutes
1 cup (250 mL) Navy beans	3 cups (750 mL)	90 minutes	90 minutes

Index

Notes

Notes